The 7 Life MIRACLES

Conquer your goals and overcome obstacles to **unlock your dream life.**

Julie Wilkes

CHANGING LIVES PRESS

The information contained in this book is based upon the research and personal and professional experiences of the author. It is not intended as a substitute for consulting with your physician or other healthcare provider. Any attempt to diagnose and treat an illness should be done under the direction of a healthcare professional.

The publisher does not advocate the use of any particular healthcare protocol but believes the information in this book should be available to the public. The publisher and author are not responsible for any adverse effects or consequences resulting from the use of the suggestions, preparations, or procedures discussed in this book. Should the reader have any questions concerning the appropriateness of any procedures or preparation mentioned, the author and the publisher strongly suggest consulting a professional healthcare advisor.

This book is intended for life empowerment purposes. Information should be interpreted and modified according to individual needs, preferences, medical history, and goals. Julie Wilkes is not responsible for any outcomes associated with this content.

Please note: Some names have been changed to respect privacy.

CHANGING LIVES PRESS
50 Public Square #1600 • Cleveland, OH 44113
www.changinglivespress.com

**Library of Congress Cataloging-in-Publication Data is available
through the Library of Congress.**

ISBN: 978-0-9894529-2-2

Editor: Shari Johnson
Cover: Involve
Interior design: Gary A. Rosenberg • www.thebookcouple.com

Printed in the United States of America

Contents

This book is dedicated in gratitude to:

My mother, who taught me to seize the day.

My father, who taught me that it is never too late.

My grandmother, who taught me how to do the right thing.

My aunt, who taught me to walk lightly and carry a big purse.

Mr. Larson, who taught me to overcome.

Dr. Taylor, who taught me to dream big.

Cody, who taught me how to love.

Gina, who taught me to "be discouraged never."

Craig, who taught me to believe, even if I don't know the outcome.

Marc, Wynn, Janine & Rich, who taught me that passion can move mountains.

Dr. Buckworth and Dr. Kirby, who taught me that sometimes, all I need is to be given the chance.

Anna, who taught me how to be strong when I felt weak.

Lisa, who taught me that true friendship lasts forever.

The Fab 7, who taught me that laughter can fix anything.

My friends and family, who taught me how much better life is when we are together.

ADDITIONAL RESOURCE RECOMMENDED TO USE AS YOU READ THIS BOOK

A Journal. Select one that has an inspirational quote on the front, a colorful tapestry in the binding, or anything that makes you look forward to using it.

Unlocking the 7 Miracles
in Your Life

Miracles. **They are all around us, all the time.** They come in all shapes and sizes. They come when we pray for them and when we don't even realize we need them. They help us in little ways. They help us in big ways. There are Miracles every day, for every person. It isn't a question of whether a Miracle is going to come into your life today; it's a matter of whether you are going to choose to see it. In fact, one may be knocking at your door right now—and when you start to see the Miracles in your life, you are empowered to conquer your goals, overcome obstacles, and live your dreams.

Children are naturally able to see Miracles in their lives. They believe in much that they don't understand. In fact, they seem happily drawn to the sparkle of the unexplained around them. They don't need the answers; they just believe. As we age, we lose sight of this sparkle, and we start to disregard the Miracles happening all around us. We stop paying attention and start rationalizing—or even ignoring—the gifts within our daily experiences. We lose our childlike way of looking at the world—one filled with excitement and possibility.

In this book I challenge you to step outside your current view and return to looking at life with your childlike eyes. I challenge you to overcome all of the things that keep you from living your life with passion and purpose. I challenge you to join me on a journey and be open to the possibility of the Miracles in your life. Once you develop the ability to recognize your Miracles, they will start to show up everywhere, and the possibilities in your life will be endless.

WHERE DO THESE MIRACLES COME FROM?

They come from you. This book just helps you tap into them.

Over the past twenty years, I have coached thousands of individuals to unlock the Miracles in their lives. As I developed my viewpoint on Miracles, I noticed the same seven areas for life empowerment in each person I worked with. I found that every person who was introduced to the concept of the Miracles was able to make profound and amazing changes in his or her life. Every single one of them. Some were already happy and were wanting to better their lives; some were looking for small nuggets of inspiration; others were looking for a full-life overhaul. Regardless of their goals, every person, in every scenario, every time, had a positive life change. They were empowered. They found happier, healthier, more joyful paths—because they learned about the 7 Life Miracles.

Many of those whom I have helped discover their Miracles have asked me to put the lessons into book form so that they can share the empowerment exponentially. That is the goal and purpose of this book—to spread the message of our personal Miracles to every person who seeks to find them.

This book is not a how-to guide. Rather, I want to share with you some of the Miracles I have experienced in my life or witnessed in others' lives. Perhaps you'll especially identify with one or two, or maybe you'll just be motivated by the possibility of them. My goal is simply to share with you some of the most inspiring lessons

I have learned through these Miracles, and I hope they will help you learn to recognize your own Miracles. All that I ask of you is to keep your mind and your heart open. You don't have to agree with me or even believe in the same things I do. Just be open to the possibilities!

This is your journey, and it is up to you to find the Miracles that have been laid in your path. But I promise you, there are Miracles just waiting for you to discover them. Consider this book a secret manual that tells you everything you need to know to find your Miracles. They will bring you greater joy, love, happiness, and success than you could ever imagine!

Life is about constant learning. It is about challenging our own thinking and searching for more—a greater understanding of our purpose, our passion, and how to make the best choices for ourselves in each moment.

So, if you are ready to begin living a life rich with everyday Miracles—phenomena, marvels, sensations, visions that bring joy and happiness to your life in amazing and unexplainable ways—then let's begin our incredible journey together.

Julie-Isms 101

Definitions
and Key Concepts

Key Concepts: The following pages provide insight into five terms I use throughout this book. Understanding them will help you understand me a little better—and how the 7 Life Miracles can help you.

1. God

2. Colors & Scents

3. Common Ground

4. LifeMap

5. Angels and Guides

GOD

Life is a spiritual journey, and, in order to write about Miracles, our journey, and our purpose, I want to give proper credit to Whom I believe makes it all possible. To me, that is God, and He is every-where—in every wind, flower, word, breath, smile, and possibility. There are, of course, many views about God, and this book is not intended to argue those views. It is meant to connect the dots among our differences and give us a united platform. I use the words

God and the Universe to unify and honor each interpretation of a Higher Power. I believe that when an idea comes from a place of love and kindness, it comes from the same Higher Power, regardless of its name. We can learn a lot from each other if we break down our barriers and remain open. I believe that God cares about how we treat the world, how we treat each other, and how we treat ourselves. By honoring these three things, we are honoring the Higher Power who gave us everything. This is how I refer to the concept of God throughout *The 7 Life Miracles*.

COLORS AND SCENTS

Colors and scents are closely tied to mindset and energy. Since this book is focused on tapping into energy and inspiration, colors and scents are natural connections. They can be a great way to help you bring the concepts to life, by taking the 7 Life Miracles off the written page and manifest them as colors and scents.

Colors

When you are surrounded by positive colors, you can feel a change in your energy. Consider working in a basement office that has no windows, walls painted a drab brown shade, and artificial light. Now consider working in a space that has big windows with a view; natural, bright light streaming in; and walls painted a beautiful shade of light blue. Your energy would be much more positive in that bright environment. Because color creates an energy source for us, I have linked a color to each of the 7 Life Miracles.

Scents

Just as colors inspire feelings, so do aromas and scents.

- The salty air may bring back happy memories of a vacation at the beach.

- Peppermint or ginger can release a headache.

- Chamomile or lavender can relax the mind.

- Fresh citrus fruit can energize the soul.

Scents have long been studied for their healing properties, so I've spent time in an aroma lab creating an inspiring combination of scents to match the energy of each of the 7 Life Miracles.

At the start of each chapter, you will see a color and several scents listed. These are for you to use in whatever way is meaningful for you. Whether you meditate with them, buy products that are associated with them to help you create an inspired space at home, or you are just aware of them, sight and smell are two powerful senses that can help you enhance your experience of unlocking the 7 Life Miracles.

Candles, oils, lotions, room sprays, and air diffusers are great ways to be surrounded with the scents of each Miracle.

COMMON GROUND

The lessons of this book accept you as you are, what you believe in, and honor your personal journey. You and I may believe in different things, but we share some important commonalities—I call this our Common Ground. This book celebrates and honors our differences, but allows us to bond on our Common Ground—providing the bridge for us to walk an inspired life together. It is important that we find this Common Ground, as too often we divide ourselves with our differences. This tends to yield a domino effect of bad energy. I don't want to contribute to the darkness in the world—I want to contribute to the light. You too? Then let's find our Common Ground so we can travel this journey together.

You might be thinking, *How does she know that we can walk a Common Ground? She doesn't know me, my family, where I came from. She doesn't know what I have been through.* You're right. I don't. But no matter where you come from, who you are, what you have gone through, and what you are currently going through, we are in this journey together; we share common threads that unite us in the 7 Life Miracles.

Recognizing that we can connect through commonalities can be one of the most empowering ways for us to grow. We have so many challenges in the world, and many of them stem from the fact we choose to separate ourselves from each other—through religion, politics, the color of our skin, or our personal preferences. If we are looking to make our lives better, we must find a way to connect with each other. Let me explain why I am so passionate about this topic.

I was fortunate to attend great school systems from elementary school through high school. While I attended highly regarded academic programs, I also had the desire to understand other life lessons not taught in class. I had a great textbook education, but I had not been challenged to understand the world outside my own sense of reality. I didn't have the exposure to other cultures, lifestyles, or people who lived even just a few miles from my zip code. It seemed to me that many people had formed stereotypes and generalizations of cultures and people they didn't understand. I saw how that broke us down—as a culture and as individuals.

As I started my high school senior year, I asked if I could devote my senior thesis (a capstone for those in a specific English class) to creating an opportunity for people to learn about each other throughout my city. My project was approved, and I enrolled at a school that was eleven miles away for one month. The demographics of this high school were different from mine, and I felt that this school would give me the chance to get outside of my comfort zone and to see how it felt to be the one who was "different." I knew that if I wanted to break down barriers, I would have to understand what it felt like to be judged and categorized.

At first, my experience at my new high school went as expected. I was judged. I was categorized. I was ridiculed. I was uncool. I was the odd man out, and I could see how my culture and life were perceived falsely and unkindly by others who didn't know me. People couldn't relate to me, didn't have a Common Ground with me, and so they dismissed me. This made life difficult.

Nevertheless, I went back each day. I tried my very best not to let the challenges of the new school get me down. I tried to keep smiling and be as friendly as I could be. Then, something extraordinary happened.

A girl asked me to sit with her at lunch. Then another girl joined us. We started to talk and laugh at the lunch table. A few others noticed and joined us. The same thing happened the next day. And the next. And eventually, I found that I had made friends.

The month passed quickly, and as I left to go back to my high school, I was sad that I had to leave so soon. I realized I had learned lessons that were quite different from what I expected. I had expected to feel unaccepted and judged because I was different. That happened, but I also found that once I discovered a Common Ground or commonality with one person—through a casual conversation and laughter at lunch—I was able to open up a door of possibility for myself. It took my being open and another person's being open to learn about each other.

When I wrote my senior thesis, I didn't focus my story on what it felt like to be the odd man out. Instead, I focused on how important it is to take the time to learn about each other. The students at the new high school were very much like the students at my high school. Perhaps they grew up in a different part of town, perhaps they dressed differently, perhaps their culture was different—but we all had a Common Ground. I found that we all just wanted to be liked by others. We wanted to have friends. We wanted to be successful in our lives (whatever definition of success meant to each of us). We wanted to enjoy life.

I loved that I had the chance to learn about another culture and lifestyle, because I grew to respect it. I also loved that I had the chance to find a Common Ground that united us and allowed us to be friends.

There are differences that we can all celebrate. I may be different from you, and you may be different from me, but we have a

Common Ground. We all want to find a way to happiness . . . to celebrate our lives and be successful, to have friends, to be accepted, to be respected, to be important to someone else, to overcome obstacles in our way, to be passionate about something, and to find simple joy.

The 7 Life Miracles guide us to those very things. Every soul who picks up this book is united on the Common Ground of a desire to be open, to learn, and be to inspired to live our best life.

No matter who you are, and no matter where you come from or what you are facing, the 7 Life Miracles will inspire and change your life in amazing ways. The secret ingredient is that we all have a Common Ground that relates to these seven concepts.

LIFEMAP

Throughout this book I refer to a LifeMap. I don't think the broader concept of a LifeMap is unique or that I am the first to talk about it. However, it is important that you understand how I define and use the term, as it is the foundation to the Miracles.

The entire story of where I got the concept of a LifeMap could warrant its own book. But in short, I learned of this concept during some significant experiences in my life. I'll go into detail later in this book about the health challenges I have had, but for explaining the LifeMap concept, I will keep it simple.

Throughout my life, my heart has stopped many times for the duration of several minutes. During such an experience, some people believe that the soul starts its ascent to Heaven. I know this is true, because I have seen the journey the soul takes. During this journey, I experienced certain things that caused me to develop the LifeMap concept.

What Is the LifeMap Concept?

I believe we are all born with a very specific purpose for our life. Our souls choose this specific path prior to being born. Each of us has a different path or LifeMap that holds the goals, dreams, knowledge, successes, and yes, even failures planned to help cultivate and grow our soul.

When you were born, a road map—your LifeMap—was placed in your imaginary back pocket. It remains there for your entire life. It is there to remind you of the journey you are on, to help you learn and grow as your soul intended. The Universe knows your Map and wants you to achieve it, so it naturally helps you along your journey.

LifeMap = Personal Road Map

On a cross-country driving trip, you might occasionally take a wrong turn, miss an exit, or get detoured. In order to continue moving toward your destination, you have to figure out 1) where you are and 2) how to get back on the path. A road map or GPS system would help you figure this out. This is the same concept as our LifeMap.

Just as a GPS system knows the route for your driving adventure, your Higher Power knows the route for your life adventure. Your Higher Power knows your LifeMap, wants you to achieve it, and will send people, experiences, and opportunities into your life to help you find your path. Your Higher Power will always help you stay on track—as long as you look for your Miracles, are open to the possibilities of your life, and are not just focused on what you think is supposed to happen. When you focus on what you think is supposed to happen, you end up spending time staring at a door that was intentionally closed. If you don't look for the open door right next to it, you may spend a lot of time stuck behind the closed door—which can lead to feeling off track in your life.

Getting Off Track

During those times in your life when you feel off track, but aren't sure why, it's likely because your soul knows the path you are supposed to be on but you aren't living that path. The soul has an amazing way of getting you back on track by giving you a tug at your heart that reminds you what you are passionate about and what you are supposed to be doing. Have you ever felt that tug at your heart? It's common to ignore it. Change seems scary and uncertain; you may not be living with passion, but it's easier than going out on a limb and taking a chance. Hear me when I say, if you feel that tug, listen to it! Something in your life is trying to tell you that you need to follow your passion. It doesn't have to be a dramatic change; it could start with something small. But listen to those tugs, that inner voice, your gut feelings—they are trying to help you live out your LifeMap and your purpose.

If you stop listening to that tug at your heart, you have given yourself permission to live in mediocrity.

You were not given a chance on earth just to live in mediocrity. You were given gifts, opportunities, and possibilities to live your passion. Life is not meant to be an easy road where you figure out how to play it safe. It's meant to be an incredible journey—full of learning, adventures, joy, relationships, and passion. We don't get an incredible adventure by settling for easy and familiar. Your life won't be a straight and easy road, but understand that those twists and turns are just a part of the journey. They teach you about yourself, how strong you are, and how much you really want something.

From this moment on, I want you to promise me one thing. Promise me this, okay? (Respond with "Yes, I promise, Julie.")

Do it. I'm waiting . . .

I want you to never, ever be okay with ignoring that tug at your heart and accepting mediocrity in your life. I want you to live the life you have dreamed of, the life you have hoped for, and the life you were born to live. I'm excited just thinking about your possibilities. It starts with your commitment to listen to that tug and understand that it is there to help you achieve your life goals. It's okay to be afraid. I'm still afraid of mine at times—until I remind myself that my LifeMap will never take me to a place I am not supposed to be. Life is about the journey, the adventure, and not always knowing the outcome. Therefore, I ask that you promise yourself never to settle in your life when you know there is more that you desire. Do we have a deal?

Good. I promise the same back to you as I attempt to follow my LifeMap. This won't be easy, and we both are going to have moments where we fall into the land of mediocrity and forget this promise.

But don't worry . . . that tug won't go away. It's your passion, it's your purpose, and it's your LifeMap. When you ignore the tug, it just gets louder and louder until you can't ignore it any longer. Sometimes it's even a little obnoxious. But there are times when we need obnoxious in order to listen. You'll find that once you get back on track—living with intention and following your passion—the doors of possibility and opportunity continue to open and guide you along.

How Your Higher Power Helps You

We aren't alone in our journey. Our Higher Power is the coauthor and supreme approver of our LifeMap and ultimately can always help us get back on track.

This is why it is not only good to pray or meditate using your favorite scripture, poems, or mantras, but also to use prayer as a way to talk to your Higher Power in an authentic dialogue. Ask Him (or Her) to show you what your purpose is . . . ask Him to remind you why you must handle some situation in your life . . . tell your Higher Power how you feel and what you think your LifeMap is all about . . . your Higher Power will answer you. Either you will leave that prayer with a sense of renewal (perhaps clarity, passion, energy, joy, calmness, a new idea) or a Miracle or sign will occur shortly, validating your prayer and reminding you of the answer that you've been seeking. These signs are things that we commonly miss or excuse for one reason or another. You have to stay open to the signs. They won't likely be glowing in neon right in front of you. They are more often subtle things, such as a recurring theme or perhaps a number that keeps appearing to you. Maybe someone says something you were just thinking or a photo appears that represents that thought. Do not ignore these moments—these are answers, guides, validations, and helpers along your incredible journey.

LifeMap Coauthors

If your Higher Power is a coauthor, who is the other author? Your soul. Your soul knows what you need to learn in order to grow in spirit, and it determines the lessons your life will live. You and God are partners in this journey.

ANGELS AND GUIDES

Angels and guides do exist. I have been visited by mine throughout my life. The first visit I remember was when I was five years old. I wasn't sure what to make of it. I ended up seeing a woman briefly appear from time to time, but I wasn't quite sure who she was or what she was doing . . . all I remember is that I wasn't afraid of her.

When I was seven years old, I was playing in my grandparents' attic and I found a box filled with old memory books, dating back to the early 1900s.

Going through the memory books, I opened to a random page and was startled when I recognized a photo on the page as the person who had been visiting me. Her name was listed below the very old black-and-white photo. She was my great-grandmother. She had passed away many years before I was born. I had never looked through those books before, and there had not been any pictures of her in my grandparents' house.

Since the age of seven, I had a clear understanding of one of my angels, and I liked her a lot. I didn't know anything about her, but I liked her energy. I felt comforted to know she was there, always looking over my shoulder.

Your Angels and Guides

I am not unique. You also have angels and guides. Everyone does.

There are many interpretations of who or what angels and guides are. In my experience, angels can take many shapes. They may be in human form as a best friend, pet, or even a stranger; they could be the soul of a loved one who has passed over and serves in spirit; or they could be a positive energy surrounding you that you can't explain, but you just know it's there. Angels visit us in physical form, spiritual form, and/or emotional form and remind us that we aren't alone. They give comfort and support.

Guides, on the other hand, are souls who are connected to your LifeMap. They are spirits or energy forces that have a purpose to help you succeed in your goals. They know your LifeMap, and they are around to give you nudges and help you stay on track.

They are with you all the time, and they will remind you of your LifeMap and how to navigate through your ups and downs. They come to you in images or simply in providing recurring thoughts, pictures, numbers, or dreams. They help direct your actions, thoughts, or choices. For example:

- Have you ever been driving and missed an exit you take often? Perhaps later you found out there was an accident on the road you missed.

- Have you called someone you haven't talked to in a while, only to discover that your help or kindness was needed at that moment?

- Have you been delayed at an airport, only to meet someone who impacted your life while you were waiting?

- Have you ever had a desire to change jobs, go back to school, or change the direction you are headed, and once you did, you found greater joy and happiness?

You may have chalked these things (or situations like them) up to coincidence, if you thought of them at all. However, if you open your mind to possibilities, you will see how your angels and guides help you every day in little and big ways.

Just because you may not see your angels and guides doesn't mean they aren't there. They can be felt through emotion, thoughts, signs, temperature changes, and desires. You may even catch an actual glimpse of one from time to time. Have you ever turned your gaze and caught something out of the corner of your eye? Or have you ever seen something and then on the double take, nothing was there?

Open your mind. Let go of your logic filter. It isn't your imagination. In fact, one of your angels is likely looking over your shoulder right now as you read this, wondering if you will notice.

(Did you just look? Good. Believe in your angels. They believe in you.)

Screech!

Hit the brakes, and let's check in.

I know . . . it's a lot to think about. You may want to go back and reread this section several times, because it's the warm-up to the rest of the book. These concepts are important to understand because I will refer to them along the way. The words in this first section alone can help you when you need a boost—a reminder of your purpose, your Miracles, and your angels. There are endless possibilities in your life, and I am just getting started.

Remember, you don't have to agree with me on everything, but I hope there are a few ideas that will capture your attention, pique your interest, or intrigue you—and that you are open to their possibility!

When you are ready, let's get started and have fun on this journey.

ORDER

How to Read This Book

You'll notice that the chapters are written in the following format:

- A title and description

- A color that represents the Miracle

- Scents that represent the Miracle

- A quotation about this Miracle

- A story that brings the Miracle to life

- A meditation to manifest this Miracle in your life

- A challenge or action for you

The Meditation and Action sections take the concepts of each chapter and ask you to make them a part of your life. You'll find these sections labeled "Unlock the Miracle" at the conclusion of every chapter.

PURPOSE

The purpose of this book is to inspire you to live out loud in your own life story. It is to inspire you to:

- Live your life with intention.

- Be open to your possibilities.

- Believe in your dreams.

- Dare you to take your intentions, possibilities, and dreams and put them into action.

Miracle 1

Embrace

Seize the day.
Make your life extraordinary.

The color of EMBRACE: Red

The scents of EMBRACE: Goji Berry,
Pomegranate

We don't have time to wait for the perfect scenario.
The perfect scenario is this very moment. If we are bold
enough to see the possibility in this moment—without excuses,
conditions, and rationalizations—we find ourselves living
extraordinary, powerful, and meaningful lives.

—JULIE

Sometimes, it takes finding out you only have a short time to live to fully grasp the concept of EMBRACING the moment and seizing the day. Most of us live each day assuming that if we don't do something today, we can most likely do it tomorrow. If we aren't bold enough to change our lives for the better this year, perhaps next year. If we don't feel strong enough to end an unhealthy relationship, it is easier to stay in it for now.

This attitude causes us to settle in our life or to play it safe. We dream of someone else's life, someone else's luck, and someone else's opportunities—when in fact that life is just waiting for us to live it! I almost named this the "Take Life by the Horns and Have a Daring Adventure" chapter, as that is truly what it is!

Playing it safe causes us to miss out on a lot of amazing, inspiring, and life-changing opportunities. When we don't feel the urgency to act on something, it is easier to put it off for another day. It can be easier to stay unhappily comfortable in our lives than to attempt to make a change that is unfamiliar and uncertain. Some of us fear that if we make the effort to change something we don't like, perhaps we will fail at the attempt and be worse off. For others, it just seems easiest not to rock the boat. We may say to ourselves, "Sure I could be happier, but I'm not miserable now. I just really don't have the time to focus on changing my life right now. Maybe next year." And then next year comes and we say the same things. Twenty years pass, and we give up on the change because "it's just too late" or worse, we forgot we even wanted it in the first place.

By living this way, we are keeping ourselves from our greatest experiences in life. All of us are given amazing gifts, talents, skills, and abilities. When we live life with intention, seizing the moment, and doing the things that we are passionate about, we are using and sharing those talents and gifts.

Remember the "tug at your heart" that I talked about in the Introduction? When you get that tug, it is because your soul is excited—it knows you are meant to do something amazing—but your body and mind hold you back. When you say no to your soul too many times, it starts to feel pushed away and ignored. You then forget your passion, forget your purpose, and choose to move forward just going through the motions of life. That tug never leaves; you just teach yourself not to hear it and then you wonder why something in your life feels "off."

You may be thinking, *I know, Julie. I have passions I've held back on because it wasn't the right time.* Or *I didn't have the money.* Or whatever the case may be. And I understand these things. We all hold ourselves back. However, I ask you from this point forward, notice when you do this. Is it money? Is it time? What is it that holds you back? Sometimes just identifying that hurdle can help you begin to "take life by the horns." But if that isn't enough, if you need a little JulieBoost, here it is.

Carpe Diem from the Heart

What if you knew that you didn't have much time left? What if you were told your days would be cut short and whatever you needed to do, you should do it now?

- Would you put things off?

- Would you worry about the things that aren't in your control?

- Would you wait to tell someone how you feel about him or her?

- Would you ignore your passion?

Me neither. I am one who grew up being told that my heart was very sick and my life expectancy was short. Each day of my life was an unexpected gift. There was not one thing that I could put off in my life. I was told I was on borrowed time and there was no promise of tomorrow. My mother has always told me, "Julie, you have to seize today, make your life extraordinary. You have to make sure you live with your heart and soul." Let me tell you my story.

My mother went hiking when she was seven months pregnant with me. She picked some beautiful flowers along the hike, and as she gathered a bunch of the most extraordinary colors and greenery, she noticed an itching feeling on her arms . . . then on her neck . . . then on her face. It turned out that she was toxically allergic to poison ivy—and there happened to be a big, beautiful cluster of it right in the middle of her fabulous bouquet.

My mother had trouble breathing and was rushed to the hospital with a toxic reaction. She must have touched her mouth at some point, and the reaction systemically spread like wildfire. The reaction attacked the umbilical cord, damaging it. From that point on, I didn't get the nutrients necessary to develop fully.

At ten months (a month overdue), my mother was losing weight and doctors were having difficulty detecting a heartbeat. Speculating that I had died in the womb and considering the health of my mom, the decision was made to deliver me via caesarian section. Alive, but with a very sick heart, within minutes of birth my heart stopped several times.

The doctors learned my heart had not fully developed. The way they described it was that it looked like "Swiss cheese." In more proper medical terms, I had a ventricular septal defect (VSD), which left me with holes in the left ventricle of my heart, and a mitral valve murmur. They felt my heart would not be strong enough to sustain life for long, and I was too small for surgery.

There was more. I was also born with epilepsy; violent allergies to formula, milk, and meat; an extreme iron deficiency; and my eyes were crossed. My mother assures me that she thought I was a cutie and even nicknamed me "Peanut." A mother sees the best in her child.

The doctors told Mom to hold me and love me, as I may only live for minutes. Minutes turned into hours, hours turned into days, days turned into weeks, and weeks turned into months . . .

At six months, a doctor wrote "Miracle" across my chart, because no one could explain how I was still alive. My first Miracle. And that word has stayed with me my entire life.

Three things kept me alive during those first six months.

1. My mother's love—I believe that our LifeMaps are the key drivers in our lives, but we all have the ability to decide if we are going to stay on our LifeMap at any moment. The LifeMap isn't a magic wand that makes things happen—we have to take action to make things happen. Also, our LifeMap doesn't just have one

path; there may be multiple paths that we can take to get to the same endpoint. The LifeMap is about guiding us toward the lessons and life we were born to live, but it recognizes that we cannot be successful without the help of others. In other words, we cannot do this alone. People are placed in our lives to help us on our adventure. That was the case with me. My mother was in my life to help me live. Her love was what I needed to continue my journey.

2. It was a part of my LifeMap—I was supposed to enter the world with challenges to teach me how to be a survivor. This skill would be something I would need and use for the rest of my life.

3. I had work left to do—I was meant to stay a little longer, perhaps to help someone on his or her path or do something that helped millions on their paths. Whatever it was, my purpose wasn't yet complete.

At the age of three, a cardiac catheterization was performed in order to determine the health of my heart. This test involves the insertion of a catheter into a chamber or vessel of the heart to give doctors a view of its health and pressures. During this procedure, the doctors found that I still had VSD (the Swiss-cheese holes), a mitral value murmur, and that my heart was working overtime to sustain life. They had not seen a heart like mine and predicted my life expectancy would be short. One doctor speculated that he did not expect me to live into my teenage years.

You probably don't remember much about being three years old. I likely wouldn't either, except that was when I learned about my heart, about my limited time, and the concept of living with intention and passion. I knew that I needed to embrace my life each day. I did some monumental and not so monumental things once I learned about my life expectancy.

First, after learning how sick my heart was and that I wasn't going to be like all of the other kids, I immediately ripped off all of my clothing and ran outside, circling our house until my mom caught me. I remember laughing so hard I had tears in my eyes—partially at my mother who was trying to catch me and partially because I was LIVING! I was having fun. I also remember rounding up our dogs and having an afternoon tea with them. I decided I needed to have a conversation with our two dachshunds about the fact that they would have to take care of my family once I wasn't around anymore. I gave them extra biscuits to thank them after they seemed to acknowledge what I said.

Knowing from the time I was a young child that I had limited time to follow my LifeMap and to achieve my life's purpose is a Miracle. I grew up learning to live urgently—and to not put things off. I remember making a rule for myself that I had to make sure my parents knew every day how much I loved them. When I awoke in the mornings, the first thing I would do is run and tell them that I loved them. Before I would go to bed at night, I would make sure the last words out of my mouth were "I love you." I remember falling asleep every night talking to God and letting Him know that if I didn't get the chance to live another day, I was happy with how I lived that day and that my parents knew I loved them. It was that simple.

As a child of three, I wasn't aware of what my entire life purpose was, at least, not consciously. But I did know one thing—my life was about love. My life was about making sure people knew how much I loved them. My life was about exploring, having fun, and learning. I had purpose . . . To love. To explore. To have fun. To learn.

As I grew, these desires became my guiding principles. Knowing I had limited time, I chose to live with passion, with peace, and with the desire to leave the world a better place—even if by just small acts of kindness. As I look back at my life, I realize that this was an invaluable way to grow up. Indeed, this was a Miracle.

Where to Begin?

Sometimes people ask me, "Where do I begin? How do I do this?

How do I live without regret and not put things off?" This is what I tell them:

Imagine that when your soul passes over, you are met at the gates of Heaven by God. He asks you about your life.

"Did you have a good life? Did you live fully? Did you learn?"

God then brings out a video of your life. You sit down and watch it together. As you watch the video of your life, if there are times that you have to explain to God why you didn't do something, if there are times that you have an excuse for not beginning something, if there are times that you aren't living with passion and joy—that is where you start.

We all will have times in life when we stall or get off track, but hopefully we learn to have less of these and more of the rich, full life experiences. Look back at your life now and study where you hesitate, where you pause, when you don't go after what you want. Start there. The key to unlocking the first Miracle is the following truth: We are never promised more than this moment. We have to make the best of life right now. It is in living with passion and finding the joy in each day—living with an exclamation point—that we find our purpose.

Some people feel they have to wait until they lose ten pounds, or until they have that perfect job, or make a certain amount of money to be able to start living. You must start today. Live as if right now is all you have. Because the truth is, this is all you have! Right here. Right now. You must embrace your life as is. There are no returns. There are no re-dos. There are no backspace or delete buttons (but wouldn't that be nice?). This is the life your soul has mapped out, and these are the lessons you are supposed to be learning. If you are leading with your passion and your heart, you will not be put into a situation that you can't handle, nor can you fail. The outcome may not be as planned, but it will be magnificent. The outcome will be what it was supposed to be.

Welcome to your first Miracle.

UNLOCK MIRACLE #1 IN YOUR LIFE!

MEDITATION

This is my moment. I am blessed beyond measure, and I am grateful. I will manifest an abundance of love and kindness. I choose to live today with passion, and intention. I choose to live urgently—with an exclamation point. I choose to listen to those tugs at my heart and follow my purpose. I will look for my angels and ask for their guidance. This is my life. I get one chance to live it—but if I live it fully, one chance is all I need. I will be my best today in every moment. I will let go of the past, make peace with the things that hold me back, and open my mind to the possibilities of each moment. I will do that which I have been putting off. I will live my life today without regret and without the hope for a re-do. I will live today on purpose.

Journal

Use a journal to record your thoughts and answers.

Step back and think about your life. Take some time to think about this.

If you were told you only had a limited amount of time in your life, what would you change?

- Your current job?

- Your relationships?

- How you give back in the world?

- How you take care of your body?

- How you treat your personal time?

- How much time you spend with your family?

- How much time you spend with your friends?

- How much time you spend at work?

Who would you call?

- Are there people you cherish with whom you have lost touch?

- Do you frequently think, *I really should call him (her)* about someone?

- Have you heard yourself use the excuse, "Life just gets in the way of staying in touch"?

What decisions would you make?

- How would you handle daily challenges?

- What would guide your process for making decisions?

- Would you shift your priorities to place emphasis on different things in your day?

You don't have to have answers or make changes for every question. Focus on a few that resonate with where you are in your life right now. If you come back to this book at another time, you may select other key areas of focus. For now, take an honest look at how you are living your life and see if there are opportunities for you to seize the day more powerfully. Pick one to five things that matter and think through how you want to approach them as you move forward in your life. Change doesn't come easily, and it won't happen just because you want it to. Writing this plan out can help bring it to life.

Sample Journal Entry

As I embrace Miracle #1, I live today with purpose and intention.

1. I incorporate my passion into my everyday work by taking on small additional assignments that allow me to use my creative skills.

2. I call one person a day to remind them how much they mean to me.

3. I work out 4–5 times a week for at least thirty minutes (no excuses).

4. I choose to eat 80% of my meals each day with a focus on energy and nutrition.

5. I do one thing a day that makes me feel good about me.

After you have written these things, record daily how you accomplished each of them.

We don't have an unlimited time to embrace the here and now—to laugh and love on a daily basis. When people wait for the "right" time, they look back and realize they missed it. Right now is the right time. Live today! Laugh today! Love today! Enjoy your life today! You'll start to notice little things happening all around you, and these are your Miracles in action.

Miracle 2

Connect

Look for your coach and pay it forward.

The color of CONNECT: Orange

The scents of CONNECT: Orange, Tangerine, Mango, Grapefruit

People come into our lives to help our souls grow, to encourage us to stay on course with our LifeMaps, and to remind us of how strong we are. They show us the way, and then encourage us to navigate for ourselves. It is up to us to look for these people, welcome them into our lives, and be open to their lessons.

—JULIE

There are people who come into our lives specifically to help us along our path. Some call them angels on earth, others call them coaches. Rest assured that whatever we call them, people will come into our lives to CONNECT with us, teach us, and show us how to be successful on our journey. Our soul created our LifeMap to include many lessons and experiences, and our soul knew we would need some help.

Chuck Taylor Shoes and a Toothpick

Because I was a kid with a severe heart problem, my mother and I feared I'd overexert myself. I was afraid to push my body as my friends pushed theirs, even during simple activities like playing on the playground. In the fifth grade, I overcame this fear with the help of one of my coaches. Mr. Larson was the fifth-grade gym teacher. From the first time I heard him talk, I was awestruck. He had a confident yet kind demeanor; funny mannerisms that made him likeable and unique; and a true, deep admiration for others. He would walk into gym class wearing his black Chuck Taylor low-top shoes, a unique heel-pause-toe stride, a toothpick sticking out of the side of his mouth, and an ever-present smile, and he would greet the class with an enormous welcome. He started every gym class with a story of one of his former students who had done something inspiring in their life. His monologue ritual went something like this:

"Terry Smith . . ." he'd say with drama and conviction, as if he were saying the two most important words in the world. He would pause and look around, pace back and forth, chew on his toothpick for a few seconds, and suddenly, just like a football coach's rally cry he would boom, "You think you are down and out? You think you can't compete? Well how about Terry Smith? Terry Smith was . . ." and then he would go on to share a story of how Terry Smith had overcome great odds to accomplish something significant.

I secretly hoped that one day he would be able to say, "Well how about Julie Wilkes?" and share a story of my climbing over obstacles to achieve more than what was expected. I felt that desire to be someone every time he shared a story. Every day he inspired us; every day he put a thought in our heads that we could be more than we were allowing ourselves to be; every day he told us that we were worthwhile and worthy of overcoming any boundaries in our paths. I began to enjoy gym class. I had never thought of myself as an athlete (the exact opposite, actually), but I looked forward to Mr. Larson's class. It wasn't just gym. It was a daily life pep rally.

That spring Mr. Larson introduced our track series—and I

became anxious. He explained that we would be paired up to race against each other in a 50-meter dash, and our progress would be documented over several weeks. Mr. Larson partnered me to run against Ryan Brockman, the fastest kid in the fifth grade. I was terrified! Mr. Larson noticed my anguish and pulled me aside to ask about it. "Wilkes. What's up?"

I shared the story of my heart problem and explained that I could not push my heart too hard. I asked him to consider partnering me up with another runner, perhaps someone slower whom I wouldn't be embarrassed to compete against.

He paused, looked at me, and smiled.

"Jules. What the heart believes, the mind and body can achieve. If you think you will fail, you will. If you think you will succeed, you will. It's that simple. Your heart is a muscle. So there is no better medicine for it to heal than for you to get out there and exercise it every day. If you want to overcome your odds, you've got to show your heart that you have a life to live, and it needs to work with you to live your life to the fullest."

The pep talk worked until we lined up for our first 50-meter dash contest the next day. I was mortified. Mr. Larson said, "Runners, on your mark, get set, go!" We started down that 50-meter-long sidewalk, and it was only seconds before Ryan left me in the dust. He finished in half the time I did. Embarrassed, I just walked to the back of the line and kept my head down, hoping Mr. Larson would see my struggle and pair me up with someone else. The next day when he called out the pairings, sure enough—I was with Ryan.

A week went by, and I continued to be humbled and frustrated. After the fifth mortifying day, I went home after school and decided that I would practice on my own. I was tired of being embarrassed and heckled by others. I asked myself, "How do I expect to be good at something if I don't practice?"

It seems that we often expect to be good at something from the start; if we aren't, we give up on it or let it get the best of us.

My first jog lasted 10 minutes. But the next day, that 10 minute-jog turned into 15. A few days later, I was up to 30 minutes. Eventually I enjoyed running so much that my mom would have to tell me when to be home for dinner. I got lost in my own thoughts as I ran through neighborhoods, parks, and streets. It was my first experience of "me-time" . . . time to focus on things that were important to me.

On the last day of fifth-grade track practice, Mr. Larson called off the pairings, and, of course, I was paired with Ryan. We were the last pair to run. As we lined up at the start, I looked over at Mr. Larson and he gave me a look that said, "I believe in you kid. Now show me what you have learned." It was a moment I will always remember. The lessons I had learned were far bigger and more important than running those 50 meters that day. My coach had taught me a lesson that my LifeMap had intended for me to learn. Mr. Larson helped me to be more than I was giving myself permission to be. I didn't need to be a passenger on my journey—I was in the driver's seat, with my faith and my coach as my navigation system! Mr. Larson empowered me to have confidence and believe in myself.

When Mr. Larson blew the whistle, I was off and running. I had a coordinated stride, my breath connected with my movement, my body felt strong and confident. It felt amazing!

I didn't win that day, at least not against Ryan, but I ran my best time, and more important, I gained lessons that had been laid out on my LifeMap.

- I possess the ability to overcome. Mr. Larson taught me that the limits in my life were self-imposed. If I opened up my heart, my mind, and my body to the possibilities in front of me, doors would open that I didn't even know existed.

- There is great value in running alongside someone who is faster. It is easy to run with people slower than we are. But when we run next to someone who is faster, we are forced to get out of our comfort zone and stretch to find greater strength than we realized we had. When we partner up with someone who pushes us, we can't help but reach new ground.

Overall Lesson

You can do anything that you really want to do. It won't happen overnight, and it won't happen by luck. But if you want something—and you are willing to break it down, work for it piece by piece, understand it, get frustrated by it, learn from it, listen to it, debate with it, chew it up, spit it out, stomp on it, make friends with it again, and then grow with it—you can achieve it. What the heart believes, the mind and body can achieve.

Don't Play It Small

Coaches will come in and out of our lives as we need them. We may not realize that we needed them, but if we look back at our lives and see all of the times when someone empowered us, believed in us, championed us, and stood up for us, there was a reason. They were placed along our paths to help us stay on our LifeMap.

Dr. Taylor is another one of my coaches. Dr. Taylor was a Leadership and Business professor at my college. He had a distinct, fun style. He asked a lot of controversial questions and encouraged students to debate them. He enjoyed playing devil's advocate to spark conversations. After taking several of his classes, I learned that he was teaching us how to stand up for our beliefs. Each time he would throw an argument out for the class to discuss and I would present my opinion, he would tell me all of the reasons my opinion wasn't necessarily correct. He would then ask if I still had the same opinion. At first, I would change my mind. However, once I realized that at times he just argued the other side to see how passionate I was about something, I learned when to hold my ground and when to be flexible. I needed to know who I was, what I believed in, and what was important to me in order to assert and own my opinions. This was an important time for me to learn to define who I was, as I would need to know that for the rest of my life.

After my second year in college, I asked Dr. Taylor to be my Advisor. He agreed, and we began to discuss where I was headed. He was one of the first people who told me I wasn't dreaming big enough. He told me I was smart, talented, kind, and capable of great things and that I could do anything that I set my mind to. He told me I was playing small and that I could do much more than I was attempting.

At first this seemed a little fairytale-ish to me, but he was relentless. He would say, "What do you want to do?" I would give him a safe answer, and he would say, "Bigger! You are far more capable! You can do anything, Julie! If you can dream it, you can do it." He would then smile at me as if he already knew where I was headed in life.

The Job Application Journey

As I was nearing graduation, I applied for a job with a company that had a reputation for being one of the best companies to work for. I didn't want to work anywhere else—just that company, and the position seemed like my dream job.

I spent hours working on my application. I used our career center templates and guidelines, I had seven people proof my writing, and I reviewed it at least a dozen times. My heart was racing, and I could hear triumphant music in my head as I marched my application letter to our campus mailbox.

Three weeks later, I received a rejection letter. I was devastated. I had failed. I raced over to Dr. Taylor's office and asked him, "What do I do? That is the only company I wanted to work for!" Dr. Taylor calmly smiled and told me to revise my application to make it stronger, and then reapply. He laughed and said, "This is part of the process, Julie." Process? To apply for a job? Or maybe it was a part of the process of learning a life lesson.

I did as he coached, and a few weeks later another rejection letter arrived in the mail. Repeat of the aforementioned panic scenario. Again, Dr. Taylor calmly told me to reapply—but he told me to go out on a limb and focus on the things that set me apart from the crowd. I sat down and stared at my "perfect" application that didn't have any errors and read like a dream. I then tossed the application in the trashcan and started over . . . again.

Instead of highlighting my high grade-point average and the leadership offices I held in college, I went a different direction. I talked about my study abroad experience. I talked about times in my life when I struggled and how I overcame those things. I talked about how I learned to dream big in college.

This application seemed to be a bit out of the ordinary. I had several people review it, and they questioned whether it was the right tone for a highly competitive company. It wasn't what I thought companies wanted to receive, but it showed my ability to overcome challenges, take some risks, and conquer big dreams. It set me apart. Dr. Taylor loved it.

This time when I submitted the application, I addressed it to an alumnus of our alma mater who worked for the company. Dr. Taylor had reminded me that we have to ask for help from others who have already walked our path.

A few weeks later (to the sound of trumpets blaring), I received an invitation to begin the interview process with this company. Eventually I was offered a job, and I accepted. I raced over to Dr. Taylor's office to tell him that I had gotten the job offer. He just smiled and had a twinkle in his eye, as though he knew this outcome in advance.

Dr. Taylor believed in me with unwavering faith and in the possibility of what I could accomplish. He taught me how to dream big—that anything is possible. These lessons are the very essence of my personal mantra today.

Just like the lessons from Mr. Larson, these lessons were carved out on my LifeMap. I would need these lessons to help me through other challenges that I would face later in my life.

As I look back at these two coaches in my life, I see a few recurring themes:

- They recognized something special in me.

- They weren't afraid to challenge me and push me out of my comfort zone.

- They didn't always tell me what I wanted to hear.

- They believed in me, even when I didn't believe in myself.

- They helped me to dream big and know that anything is possible.

Look for your coach (or coaches). You might feel that asking for help is a weakness. You might feel the desire to be independent and figure things out on your own. Nevertheless, the strongest individuals are the ones who ask for help, offer help, and enjoy the journey of learning with others.

Your coach will help you stay connected to your passion and your purpose. That person will remind you how fabulous you are, but won't be afraid to challenge you. Your coach will help you learn the lessons intended for you—will help you through the little things and will help you through the big things.

Pay It Forward

Sometimes a coach comes into our lives to help us so that, in turn, we can help others. We learn these lessons so we can be a coach for someone else. Life is not just about our own journeys; it is about helping others along theirs as well.

You may think, *I'm just trying to figure out my own life. How can I help others?* Each of us, at every point in our lives, has a gift to share. While all of our LifeMaps are different, we are all are striving to learn:

- How to overcome challenges

- How to forgive others

- How to leave the world a better place

- How to be our best in any situation

None of us will master these things. Many yogis believe that if you think you have perfected yoga, you should try something else, because you didn't get the lesson at all. The same is true here. We don't have to wait to be an expert or for our life to be running smoothly (does it ever?) to pay forward on our gifts. Life is simply a constant journey of twists, turns, ups, and downs. And just as someone is here to help us through a tough time, we are here to show someone else the way.

I debated which example to use to highlight this concept. There are countless examples of inspiring celebrities who had a coach help them grow to greatness and are now paying forward by helping others. I am sure you can think of some right now. While there are great examples of celebrities who pay forward, I decided to go in a different direction. I chose to share the story of an ordinary young man who did an extraordinary thing.

Rory

I met Rory when he was fourteen. As a freshman, he was the captain of his varsity football team and loved playing sports of all kinds, especially baseball. He had the charisma of an evangelical preacher and the kindness of a saint. He also had the good looks of a model, but was humble and modest. He could make anyone laugh and loved spending time with his family, friends, and teammates. He seemed to have it all. I have never met anyone quite like him.

Shortly after football season ended that year, Rory was diagnosed with a rare form of cancer. Unfortunately, the prognosis for this type of cancer wasn't good. Rory understood he would need to undergo a number of tests, treatments, and procedures. He also knew the likelihood of his dying from this disease. His journey was difficult. Months of treatments didn't work. Painful procedures frustratingly failed. His body became weaker. His leg had to be amputated. He lost his hair. He gained forty pounds of water weight. His entire body broke out in a red rash due to an infection from his amputation. The doctors were unable to treat the infection because of the cancer medications in his system.

When I visited Rory in the hospital, he would smile and tell jokes. I asked him where his optimism came from and he said, "My football coach always taught me that we can be down, but we just can't be out. We have to get back up again every time we get knocked down. Every time. Winning doesn't come from staying on two feet; it comes from learning how to stand back up. Some hits are going to be harder than others, but we have to just keep moving forward. We just have to keep going and get back up! So, I am just doing what he told me. Every day, I just have to get back up."

I smiled, knowing this young man had a special soul and a special purpose.

One day, I asked him how he felt about losing his leg. I assumed it might be good to talk about, no matter how difficult. Prior to cancer, his goal had been to become a professional baseball player. Now, that was out of reach.

He looked at me, puzzled. "What do you mean?"

Feeling uncomfortable, I brought up his goal of being a professional baseball player.

Without hesitation, he said, "Oh, I'll still be one. I'll just play for the paraplegic league. I will be their best player!"

Many people would allow their pain, their frustration, their disappointment, their challenges to get the best of them—to shatter their goals and break them down. But not Rory. In fact, he not only stayed positive and optimistic, but he also decided to use his journey as a way to inspire others.

As he sat in his hospital room, he began blogging about his experiences. He talked about the details of his illness, his treatments, and his prognosis. In every single entry, he spoke with humor, energy, and a positive outlook. A few months later, right before Rory passed away, he asked his readers to stay strong and never give up what they believe in. He mentioned that his friends, family, coach, and team had helped him to be strong. They were the ones who coached him through his challenging time.

At my last visit, we all knew the end was near. I tried hard not to cry in front of him. I took a few deep breaths before walking into the room and put on my best smile. As I turned the corner and walked in, I saw him lying nearly lifeless on the bed and my eyes welled up. My throat had a hard, burning feel to it, and I was sick to my stomach. His eyes were closed, so I thought he was sleeping. I closed my eyes, trying to get my emotions under control, and felt warm tears run down my face.

I then heard a voice say, "Why are you crying?" Embarrassed, I looked up to see Rory—weak, yet smiling at me. I didn't know what to say to him, and so I just smiled back. He said, "You know this was my purpose. I have lived out the plan I came here with. You know that, Julie. I know you do. My soul is happy. My life is complete. Carry on my messages. Remember to always get back up no matter how hard you get knocked down. That's what my coach taught me, and that's what I share with others."

Once he passed, I spent a lot of time thinking about Rory's life, his purpose, and his journey. I reread his blogs and noticed something. I saw that other children and adults who had cancer (and other grave illnesses) were following his blog. In fact, thousands of people were following him and hundreds were subscribing to his blog each day—even after his passing! I read the comments they posted and found that many of these individuals were relying on Rory's blogs to help them get through their journey. Some commented that his positivity was contagious. Others mentioned how they felt stronger after reading his words and they would choose to "get back up." They all used Rory as a coach to get them through their difficult time. The blog was a legacy he left behind—so that others could learn from him and stay strong during their most difficult days.

I realized that his purpose in life wasn't to overcome his illness, but to show us how to live life to the fullest. His purpose was to show all of us how to stay positive and be joyful throughout our journey. His life was about being strong and resilient, even when challenged and uncomfortable. His life taught us how to emulate those qualities in our own lives. His support system lovingly helped him through his tough time, and then he paid it forward by sharing his life lessons with others. He thanked many of us for being his teachers, but in fact, he was ours. He taught us how to get back up.

Find your coach. Embrace their lessons. Pay those lessons forward. This unlocks another Miracle in your life.

UNLOCK MIRACLE #2 IN YOUR LIFE!

MEDITATION

My life's journey is made of straight roads, twists, turns, bumps, peaks, valleys, and mountains. They are all perfectly positioned along my path to follow my purpose. I am not meant to navigate these by myself. People have been placed along my journey to guide, assist, teach, show, and empower me to be my best in each situation. I will be open to receiving help from others and will value the experience and life lessons they have to share. I will also seek out opportunities to share my life lessons with others. And I will always remember to get back up, each day—with the help of others.

Journal

Use a journal to record your thoughts and answers. Practice CONNECTING the life you want to live.

Step back and think about your life. Take some time to think about these questions:

- Who has coached you along your journey?

- What lessons have they helped you learn?

- Have you thanked them?

- Is there a way you can pay forward on their lessons?

- Is there a lesson you are learning right now that might help others?

- Are you overcoming a struggle and could be an inspiration for someone else who is also going through something similar?

- Can you do anything to share what you have learned with others?

While we sometimes feel invincible, we cannot get through life on our own. We need our guides, our coaches, our friends, and our support system to be there with their words of encouragement, their honesty, and sometimes just a twinkle in their eye to remind us that we truly have everything we need to be successful.

If you came up with a list of people who have been your coaches or are currently coaching you through a challenging time, make sure that you thank them. Do it in the next 24 hours. Let them know what their kindness and support mean to you! If one of your coaches is no longer alive, thank them through a prayer or an act of kindness. Just a little bit of gratitude can be a great way to create a frequency of happiness around you in their honor.

Miracle 3

Create

**Create your own canvas—
create the life you want to live.**

The color of CREATE: Light Green

The scents of CREATE: Cucumber,
Awapuhi

*What would your life look like if you had the choice to write
your own script? Well, good news—you do write your own script,
so you'd better get started. You have a lot of life to create!*

—JULIE

Take a few deep breaths. Clear your mind. Give yourself
the privilege of finding peace in this moment. Do not read
any further until you are able to feel a sense of relaxation.

This chapter is focused on a growth process I call CREATING
Your Own Canvas. This means, create the life you want to live—not
the one that someone else wants you to live or that you have been
living due to circumstance, but the life you want to live. It means
to wipe the slate clean and CREATE what you want. This requires
you to let go of the past, let go of the habits that don't serve you,

let go of the stories you have made up in your mind, and start with a blank canvas that you are then able to fill with passion and joy. This canvas represents the image you want to paint of your life. To achieve your dreams, you have to let go of the things that have not worked for you and create a fresh perspective of where you are headed.

While this may sound simple, it isn't.

We are creatures of habit. As much as we'd like to believe that we are open to new perspectives and ideas for our lives, most of us find security and stability in routines, processes, and familiar paths. If you don't think this is true, then ask yourself why you always take the same route to work every day or why you have a specific, nightly order to getting ready for bed (brush teeth, wash face, etc.). Letting go of old habits can be difficult because they are familiar and comfortable.

Attempting to do something different taxes our brains. It is new, it is uncertain, and it is challenging. Our brain activity is extremely high when we work to accomplish a new task. Yet once we have performed a task for a while, the memory of it is formed in the deepest part of our brain where habitual memory patterns live. We no longer have to think when we are trying to perform that act, because the brain knows how to do it intrinsically.

Here is an example of how this concept works:

1. (New) Dinner tonight. Try a new recipe for your main meal.

2. (Habit) Dinner tonight. Cook a meal you make often.

Process of trying the new recipe:

1. Look up the recipe.

2. Buy the ingredients.

3. Read the directions several times.

4. Measure each ingredient.

5. Keep checking it as it bakes.

6. Read the instructions again, wondering if you forgot anything.

7. Create a back-up plan if it doesn't turn out.

Process of cooking a familiar recipe:

1. Mindlessly combine ingredients and bake, trusting that it will turn out as it always does.

When you are familiar with something, the memory of it is in your brain pattern. Your brain goes on autopilot and does what it knows.

Your life often relies on this cycle. Using habits as a way to structure daily living can be a good thing. Positive habits can help you work in the most efficient manner, stay organized and calm, be your best, and make confident decisions that support your goals and aspirations. You can do all of these things without having to give much thought to them, because they have become a part of how your brain works.

However, habits can also have a negative effect. If you have formed a habit that causes you to lose your confidence, feel defeated, or get off track, then it is important to understand how this process works so you don't keep repeating a vicious cycle. You can do these things without much thought, because these bad habits also become ingrained in your brain patterns.

Break the Habit

New Year's resolutions are great examples of this type of habit. Some people start each year by stating, "This is going to be my year to quit smoking" or "I am really going to lose those ten pounds this year." But in 365 days, these same people make the same declarations. Why?

It takes a lot of effort to think about doing something new. Look at how many steps it took to bake a new recipe—try changing an entire aspect of your life! Not only does it take a lot of thought and brain activity to make this change, but the change takes consistent practice in order to become a habit.

I have been working with one of my clients for years. At the start of our relationship, she called me on New Year's Day and said, "Julie, this is it. I am ready to go. No excuses. Let's do this." We sat down and discussed her goals, created a three-month plan, and then we met several times a week to ensure she was on track. Within a month or so, she started canceling appointments, forgetting to report her physical activity, and then eventually went MIA (missing in action). Three hundred and thirty-five days later, as the New Year rolled around, I got another phone call from her, "Julie, this is it. I am really ready to go."

At the beginning of year three of this vicious cycle, I decided that we would not be successful if we continued to repeat the same pattern. She had it ingrained in her brain that she would start something, get sidetracked, and never accomplish it. She subconsciously sabotaged herself, because she had always failed in the past. As silly as it may sound, she was comfortable with failing because it was what she knew how to do—it was the habit she had formed over the years. It would take a great effort of thought, brain activity, and commitment to create a different outcome, because this is the pattern she had created for her life.

As a life coach and personal trainer, I was not comfortable with one of my clients failing. While success was up to her, I had to think of a different way to work with her. I had to shake things up so that she didn't repeat her patterns and end up failing yet again.

Year three of our training program began by spending time discussing her past, what had gotten in her way of being successful, and identifying those recurring patterns. What she found surprised her. She realized that while she wanted to accomplish healthy lifestyle habits, she had been raised in an environment that gave her permission to get off track. For example, when she did well in school, her mother would bake a huge meal. When she had relationship problems, her family would console her by watching movies and eating junk food. When she had stress, her dad would say, "Have a cigarette." She found that her social circle had taught her to resort to unhealthy habits as a way to get through stress, and that had become the habitual pattern throughout her life.

Now that we understood this, we had to figure out how to let go of those unhealthy habits and start fresh by creating the habits, life, and opportunities that she dreamed of having. I had my client create her own canvas using the exercises outlined in this chapter. She had to start by clearing her canvas of the colors that impeded her ability to be powerful. In other words, she had to get rid of the stuff that weighed her down and kept her from moving forward.

I am happy to share with you that after five years she has sustained her goal weight, is stronger and more energized than she has ever been in her life, exercises four times a week, and is a positive and powerful person who not only accomplished her health goals, but allowed that positive practice of good habits to transcend into other aspects of her life as well.

She had to start by clearing out the past—getting rid of the old excuses, stories, and habits, and replace them with powerful, positive, consistent choices that allowed her to live the life she dreamed of . . . and the same is true for you.

When you want to live your best life, it is important to be able to let go of the things that aren't helping you become powerful and find the things that do. Use the following exercises to help you tap into this concept and create your own canvas. These exercises will ask you to examine your current life, identify what you don't need, and create the masterpiece you want.

Exercise 1   Viewing Your Current Canvas

Before we can make the first brushstroke on our clean canvas, we have to figure out who we are and where we are in our life—without filters, logic, or the impressions of others.

Consider every action, thought, and moment of your life to be a brushstroke and a color that you add to your own personal canvas.

You've been creating your own personal canvas for years—in fact, since the day you were born. Have you ever stopped to look at it? Have you ever stopped to take a snapshot of what your life looks like right here and now? Well, you are about to.

Read through the following and select a few key questions. These are the things to consider as you begin to think about where you are in your life and your current canvas:

- How do you feel today?

- What makes you happy?

- How do you feel about yourself/your choices in life?

- How do you handle stress? Do you have an outlet?

- How do you spend your time?

- What are your passions?

- What do you enjoy doing? How much time do you actually spend doing that?

- What makes you laugh? Do you laugh every day?

- Do you work? Do you go to school? Do you take care of your family?

- Do you have hobbies?

- Do you volunteer?

Close your eyes and take some deep breaths to clear your mind. Focus on the sound of your breath. Focus on the energy in your body. Focus on the lifting of your rib cage on the inhalation and the relaxing of your shoulders on the exhalation. Focus on freeing your mind from the chatter, worry, anxiety, self-doubt, or other "stories" that you have on your mind. Free yourself from distractions. Think about a few of those questions and formulate an image, a narrative, an understanding of where you are in your life right now.

Translate those ideas into colors and shapes. If you were to paint the colors of your life onto a canvas, what colors would they be at this moment? Bright vibrant colors? Dark, gloomy colors? A little of both? Energetic swoops of brushstrokes or fast, rigid lines on the canvas? Can you get a feel for how you think of your life right now?

Before we begin any journey, it is important to take inventory of where we are and what we bring with us. It is important to understand our current canvas, so we can decide what we want to create as we begin with a clean one.

Exercise 2   Uncoloring Your Canvas

Each day we wake up with the lessons and experiences of the previous day in mind. We determine what we carry with us. Unfortunately, we sometimes carry the negative things that weigh us down and keep us from being our best.

There are many reasons why we do this. Perhaps it is easier to go through the same routines each day, because they are familiar and comfortable; or we don't even realize that we are welcoming toxic and negative stuff into our lives; or we think that we are in a place where we have to accept life as is.

If you have negative colors that chronically lurk on your canvas, I am giving you permission right here, right now, to strip these away from your masterpiece. In the first exercise, I asked you to think about your life and determine where you are currently. Exercise 2 is a continuation of that thought. I want you to think about any road-blocks, obstacles, and unnecessary anxiety or worry in your life.

- Are you surrounded by toxic people or a toxic environment?

- Does your own inner voice have a toxic thread to it?

- Have previous experiences built up walls around who you really are?

- Do you have an outlet for stress?

- Is there anything weighing on your mind that you can't seem to free yourself from?

Take a few deep breaths and let your stream of consciousness take control. Just let your mind think out loud without quieting it, filtering it, or stopping it. Did you uncover any of the negative brushstrokes on your canvas? Chances are, you have some. We all do. It is amazing how just the addition of a few dark brushstrokes can turn a beautiful, energetic, and inspiring painting into a dark, murky one. The same is true in our lives. Just a few negative feelings, toxic people, or stressful situations can change how we interpret our life. There are so many people who have a wonderful life—a beautifully colored canvas—but there are one or two dark, ugly brushstrokes on it, and those are the colors they focus on. But I have a solution:

Let them go. Let them go. LET THEM GO!

(Just want to be sure you don't skip over those three little words.)

If you have any colors on your canvas that aren't helping you live a wonderful life, you don't need them. They are not helping you achieve your purpose and your passion. I give you permission to decommission them from your life. You are starting with a fresh canvas, and those things will not come with you.

That doesn't mean you have to cut people out of your life or disregard the hurt or frustration of your past. Rather, you will choose to perceive these things differently as you move forward. Instead of letting someone break you down, allow yourself to create distance from that person or at least know that whatever he or she says or does is not truth—not YOUR truth.

Visually picture those things leaving your life. As you erase them from your canvas, give yourself permission to live a happy life, free from toxicity and negativity.

Is it that simple? Yes and no. I realize that these unwanted colors may have been building up for years. It will take some time, some trials, and some patience to remove these colors from your life. However, recognizing that they are present and that you do not want them anymore is a great starting point.

Once you have done this and understand that you have a grip on the paintbrush that can take them off your canvas, you will start noticing small ways to redirect your actions and thoughts. When one of them starts to resurface, you will be able to recognize it and let it go.

Exercise 3   Determine Your Colors!

You've taken some time to think about who you are today, what you want to bring to your clean canvas, and what you don't. Now it's time to start dreaming. This is my favorite part. Start by picturing a blank, white canvas.

Close your eyes and spend some time clearing the chatter. Let go of the past and imagine your fabulous future. Do not let logic, money concerns, the doubts of others, or anything else interfere with your dream. Be honest about what you want. I am not encouraging you to dream unrealistically—dream about what excites your passions and fuels your soul.

As a reminder, at the end of this chapter, you will have the opportunity to spend more time practicing these exercises.

Picture the life you would like to live ten years from now. What year will that be? What age will you be?

- How will people describe you?

- What is important to you?

- Where do you live?

- What do you do?

- What is your home like?

- Are you happy?

- With whom do you spend your time?

- What is your day like?

- Can you see yourself laughing?

- At what time do you wake up each morning?

- What is the first thing you do?

- Can you picture the place where you spend your time?
- What is your daily routine (work, house, school, kids, etc.)?
- Can you see the path you walk for exercise each morning?
- When you go to sleep, how do you feel?
- Are you living with passion?

Spend some time lingering on your daydream for a while. Enjoy where your mind takes you and have fun thinking about the possibility of your future.

Once you have a picture of your life ten years from now, it is important to write that vision down. It will give you direction as you start to make choices today. Take your time. Reflect honestly about your dreams. Not just what looks good on paper, but the person you truly aspire to be and the life you want to live. And don't worry; your vision may change over the next ten years, but it is important to have something to help you set the stage today. This creates the "big picture," which is the compass for your goals and decisions.

Exercise 4   Setting Goals to Bring Your Colors to Life*

Once you have your vision—an actual image of your goals and dreams—it is important to have specific steps that will help you to be successful. Studies show that focusing on one big dream can be difficult, but small steps and mini-goals can keep the passion, excitement, and focus on track.

It is important to recognize that the choices and steps you take

---

* My goal-setting model was derived from a variety of life experiences and teachings that I blended into my own coaching tool. These concepts were modified over time, as I learned what helped my clients to be most successful. They were originally inspired from goal-setting workshops and training from lululemon athletica, Dr. BJ Fogg, and Wellcoaches.

today will compound over time to thrust you into your ten-year dream. If the goals you are making right now do not align with your ten-year vision, they may be taking you off track.

Start by thinking of your life in time increments—perhaps one year at a time. Set milestones for each year or increment leading up to your ten-year vision. Your focus could be personal, professional, or both.

Once you have this mapped out, it is important to think about smaller steps you can take right now to achieve your one-year milestone(s). Write measureable, specific goals. Organize your goals around a weekly, monthly, or quarterly basis.

Example of a professional vision/milestone timeline and quarterly goals:

Date: 1/1/2013

STEP 1: Vision: Ten years from today I am a self-sufficient lecturer, author, and wellness studio owner in California.

STEP 2: Timeline

Timeframe	Milestones
1/1/2014 (1 year)	Release my first book.
1/1/2016 (3 years)	Give my 100th lecture on my first book.
1/1/2018 (5 years)	Give my 200th lecture on my first book; release a second book.
1/1/2020 (7 years)	Give my 300th lecture on my books and rent space for wellness studio.
1/1/2023 (10 years)	Have more requests to lecture than I can fill; release my third book and own my own studio in California for wellness programs, lectures, yoga, and meditation.

STEP 3: Goals – Year 1

Milestone: Release my first book.

Timeframe	Goals
Months 1–3	Write my first 4 chapters.
Months 3–6	Write my final 4 chapters.
Month 6–9	Proofread book; send to editor; work with cover designer.
Months 9–12	Create press kit for book; review final version.
1 year	Send to publisher.

When your vision, milestones, and goals are mapped out, you have created your guidebook for success. You have shown yourself that your dreams can be a reality.

Want It!

Oh, yes—one more thing that I need to mention . . .

Your vision, milestones, and goals SHOULD BE WHAT YOU REALLY WANT! Often, we set goals for something we don't really want, but we think we want it because it sounds good.

When coaching a client, I ask them to tell me about their vision for their life. Then I ask them to tell me what steps they are taking to align with that vision. Many times I find that people are focused on something that sounds good, but not on what they want—their journey isn't much fun and they easily get off track.

The following is an actual, written goal from one of my clients:

3-MONTH GOAL: Run 4 x a week—30 minutes each time.

I have tried this in the past and have failed, but this is the year I am going to do it!

As I look at this goal, I see a few things:

- She has set a specific, measurable goal. Good.

- I don't know why she wants to achieve this. (What milestone is this working toward?)

- She has had trouble in the past. (Something is getting in the way.)

As I asked questions about the motivation for this goal (milestone), she shared how she wants to do something that is just for her, that helps her lose weight, and that can take her outside of the house. I also learn that she hasn't been successful in the past because she doesn't really like to run.

So, take a moment and think about this scenario. How would you coach her?

Exactly! Help her to see that running is not the milestone—the milestone is to get out of the house, be healthy, and find something she can commit to and enjoy that is just for her. If the goal of running hasn't worked the last five times she has tried it, maybe it's time to try something else that can help her reach the same milestone.

Do you see how that works? It is not just about setting goals; it is about understanding what you want to achieve by setting them. There are many ways to accomplish an outcome. If one doesn't work, find one that does.

That's why I encourage you to start by dreaming of what you want your life to be ten years from now. Picture what you want and then work backward, setting up smaller goals along the way that pave the way for your vision. Set goals for things you actually want to accomplish.

Spend as much time in this exercise as you need. Focusing on your vision, milestones, and goals takes a while. Some people can complete this activity in a few hours; others take several weeks or longer. Don't rush yourself. Enjoy discovering how amazing you are and how much possibility lies before you.

Exercise 5   Creating Your Canvas

I ask all of my clients to complete exercises 1–3 before I begin working with them. These exercises not only ask them to think about their life in meaningful ways, but they enable me to coach them better, and they help break down the typical barriers that get in the way of accomplishing goals. After my students have mapped out their goals, passions, dreams, and planned actions (Exercises 1–4), I can customize my approach, taking into account the best way each person learns. Typically, I've found two different types of goal-setters: 1) tracking journalers and 2) hands-on learners.

For the journaling goal-setter

Fifty percent of my students will map their dreams, goals, and objectives in a journal. Using Exercise 4 as their guide, they have everything they need to plan and execute their goals. People in this group tend to be self-disciplined, they like using the tracking tools, and they are inspired by having a plan.

If you relate to this fifty percentile, then congratulations! You have started your new canvas and are on your way to filling it with amazing colors and shapes. Please use your journal as your personal guide and tracking tool to stay on track with your monthly, quarterly, and yearly goals so that your ten-year dream becomes your reality.

For the hands-on goal-setter

The other fifty percent of my students need a different incentive or inspiration to bring these dreams, goals, and actions to life. Written goals and actions are not a strong enough first step for them. This group tends to be comprised of those individuals who are hands-on kinesthetic learners—that is, they have to feel or see something to make it real.

For this type of inspired soul, I have come up with a few ways to help bring their canvas to life. In the next few examples, I will show creative, organizational, and meditational ways to start with a clean canvas (let go of the toxic patterns and habits) and begin filling it with all sorts of colors and possibilities.

If you are more of a kinesthetic learner, one of these exercises may be a great way of bringing your goals and objectives to life. You may also benefit from journaling.

Kinesthetic Learners—Option 1

For the Creative Learner:
The Art of Bringing Your Goals to Life (Goal-painting)

Items needed: a blank canvas, brushes, water, paint

Some people are inspired by creating a visual representation of their goals. Our unconscious minds can speak a language that our conscious minds filter. Being creative allows us to tap into that unconscious side of our brain. I have taught thousands of people this goal-painting activity, and now I am bringing this to you—to help you create your own canvas.

1. Begin with a blank canvas.

2. Any size or style will do. Go to a craft store or an art store to find one that appeals to you. You can also use plain paper.

3. Have some paints and applicators available, such as water colors, acrylics, or oil; brushes, wedges, or sponges. List your one-year milestone(s):

   • Write down 3–10 goals that align with your one-year milestone(s).

   • Associate a color with each of those goals. For example, your goal could be "I want to write a book this year," and you use purple to represent this goal (colors can have symbolism or not).

4. Play your favorite music (it draws out your creative side).

5. Begin with one goal per color; make a few brush strokes or designs on your canvas with that color.

6. Move on to the next goal/word and color.

7. By the time you are complete, you will have a painting that symbolizes your goals, your words, and your energy.

8. Varnish with a spray or lacquer, if you want to protect it.

9. Hang or place somewhere that will remind you of your goals.

10. You may want to include an outline with goals/words/colors on the back of the canvas, as a reminder of the painting's meaning.

11. There is no need to paint a picture; feel free to be abstract. Just placing color on canvas in emotional and inspiring ways can translate into placing color into your life in emotional and inspiring ways. Abstract is beautiful.

I've had many clients do this exercise. While some are uncomfortable with it at first ("I'm not an artist." "I don't know how to paint."), if you put on some good music and let go of preconceived notions, you can't help but create something symbolic, meaningful, and beautiful.

Goal-Painting for Everyone

I tried this exercise with my grandmother. She had been feeling restless and anxious.

I brought her a blank piece of paper and asked her to write down five things that make her happy. I then asked her to associate a color with each of those things. At first she hesitated, but then she started to write.

This is what she wrote:

What Makes Me Happy	Color Associated
Baking	Brown
Taking walks	Green
Making people smile	Red
My family	Purple
My faith/church	Yellow

I poured paint of each of those five colors into little cups and gave her various painting tools. I told her to think about each thing that made her happy as she painted.

Again, she hesitated. "Julie, I am not a painter. Mine won't be any good." My response was, "Gram, that is the cool thing about art. It's your own self-expression, so no matter how it turns out, it will be perfect!"

She started to paint. And paint. And paint. When she finished, my eyes filled with tears as I saw a beautiful abstract painting that told the story of what makes my grandmother happy. She looked at me and said, "In my eighty-seven years, I have never painted before. Wow! That was fun!"

I told her that she was an artist, and she smiled.

On that day she was not only reminded of the things that make her happy, but she also realized a new talent that she didn't know she had—and that gave her confidence. Painting enabled her to get her mind off the things she could no longer do and created a new canvas of focus on all of the amazing things that she had in her life that made her happy.

She let go of her past version of happiness and was able to look into new possibilities for her future. She knows she cannot do every-thing that she used to do, but now she celebrates the things she can.

Sometimes, all you need is permission to let go of those negative feelings—worry, anxiety, fear, insecurity—to realize how much you have right in front of you. That can happen when you physically and metaphorically create a clean canvas in your life—and fill it with any colors that are meaningful and purposeful.

Kinesthetic Learners—Option 2

For the Organizational Learner: Fresh Start In-house

A clean canvas can be created on something other than an actual canvas. How you organize your home or work space is directly related to how you see your life. If you want to create a clean canvas or embark on a new journey, begin by changing or reorganizing your living/working space.

You can clean and organize your home or office, move furniture around, paint your walls, change an accent color—anything that gives off a bit of a different vibe will allow you to make a fresh start. Your surroundings strongly influence how you feel, so it is important to make sure you surround yourself with positive inspiration and a space that invites possibility into your life. Often, all it takes is a little external change to inspire the change within us.

Kinesthetic Learners—Option 3

For Physical Learners: Fresh Start Through Meditation

Another way we can start fresh with a clean canvas is through meditation. Many people tell me they struggle with meditation. If that's you, don't worry, you aren't alone! It is very difficult for us to slow down and teach ourselves just to be. We are constantly doing—working, taking care of our family, cleaning, cooking, calling, texting, emailing. I understand. I can't promise you that meditation will be easy for you, at least not at first. But if you are interested in starting with a clean canvas and want to begin simply, then give it a try.

Meditation works because you free yourself from distractions. Once you have become comfortable with meditating, you can literally allow yourself to come into this distraction-free state anywhere, even in the busiest and/or loudest of places. At first, I encourage you to begin meditating in a quiet space where you feel safe and comfortable. There are no absolute rules to meditation, but I have included an exercise that can get you started. You may want to read through this several times and then practice doing it. The first few times you try it, you will likely be uncomfortable and feel impatient with yourself. Slow down. Breathe. Continue to practice. Give yourself a few weeks of practicing this for five minutes every day. You may find your true canvas colors with the art of meditation, and many times, once you've cleared your canvas, your LifeMap begins to show you your path.

SAMPLE MEDITATION

Sit, lie down, or get into any position you like. For a few minutes, just breathe and notice your breath coming in and out of your body. Feel your rib cage expand and then release. Feel the pressure that leaves your body on every exhale. Continue smooth, slow breathing until it becomes easy, almost thoughtless.

Notice how your body feels. Be aware of your senses. Are there any places that are holding on to stress? Tension? Anxiety? Worry? The past? An insecurity? A frustration? Anger? Resentment? Any of these things can be toxic to the soul. Let them go.

Focus on the energy in your body and begin to release and relax every muscle.

Start at the bottom of your feet: Breathe in and as you exhale, feel your arches relax. Move up to your calves and shins, and as you exhale, let any tension dissipate. Move up to your quadriceps and hamstrings (upper leg) and release and relax them. Continue to move throughout your body—to your hips, lower abdominals, lower back, rib cage and upper abdominals, upper back, shoulders, chest, back of the neck, back of the head, top of the head, forehead, eyelids, cheeks, nose, mouth, chin, front of the neck, shoulders, biceps and triceps (upper arms), forearms, wrists, palms, and fingers.

Each time you focus on one of these muscles or body parts, breathe in a deep slow breath, and as you exhale, feel tension release. Once you have gone through your entire body, notice if there are any places that still harbor resistance. This resistance could be in your muscles (tension), your mind (can't stop thinking about something), or your heart (anger, sadness, frustration). If you discover you have a place that is holding on to resistance, spend more time specifically focusing on releasing that tension. With every exhale, give yourself permission to let go.

Do this as long as you need to, until you have relaxed your entire body. This is a cleansing activity—it allows you to open your mind and get rid of the things that are keeping you back or breaking you down. Once you feel truly relaxed and open, focus on finding peace with just being present. Sometimes I repeat a mantra to help me keep my mind from wandering. My favorite mantra to use is "So Hum" (Sanskrit meaning, "I am"). It is the closest state of an unfiltered, unconscious mindset you can have, outside of sleeping.

Once you bring yourself back from your meditation, you tend to have a sense of clarity, relaxation, or realization of something profound. Or sometimes you just feel good. Regardless, you return for the better. This is a physical way to let go of the walls, barriers, and hurdles that you impose on yourself. When practiced over time, meditation can be a de-stressing, mind-opening, possibility-revealing, canvas-cleaning exercise that brings you to some of your greatest self-taught lessons.

God Hands You a Menu

One of the most common reasons we do not do something is because we are afraid of failure—a fear usually based on past failure or rejection. When we start with a clean canvas, we take the lessons out of those experiences, but we don't let them define us. A clean canvas allows us to start over, but also invites us to bring along anything from our past that we love. Our clean canvas allows us to live in the life we have chosen, with the colors, movements, energy, and happiness that we desire.

It's almost as though God hands you a menu and asks you to

select what you want and don't want in your life. It can be that simple. Changes won't happen immediately, but they will happen if you have a plan and stay committed to that plan.

Whatever intrigues or is in accord with your soul, even if it is out of your comfort zone, is worth trying. If you are inspired to paint a new canvas in your life, clean house, spend some time in meditation—or any other canvas-cleaning activity—you can wipe away the old and start new. You have to spend some time deciding what you want and don't want in your life; what you are willing to release and what you believe are your true colors. You have a legacy to leave the world, and you can't let yourself get weighed down by the past.

You have to know what you want to get what you want, so be specific, and don't let someone else dictate your worth, your passion, your value, or what you offer to the world. Those are yours to define, with the help of your Higher Power.

I challenge you to create your own canvas today. Create the life you dream of; let go of the things you don't. Radiate the colors of your soul.

UNLOCK MIRACLE #3 IN YOUR LIFE!

MEDITATION

My life is a masterpiece. I choose the colors and brushstrokes that make up my canvas. I have the ability, at any time, to start fresh and create a clean canvas, simply by focusing on the things that are most important to me and letting go of the things that are not important. If something doesn't help me to be powerful, amazing, and inspired, I do not need it. Every day is a new day, and I choose to live with creativity, positivity, and empowerment. Anything is possible, and if I can dream it, I can do it. I have a plan, and I am focused on it. There will be days I get off track, but I always have the opportunity to start fresh the next day, let go of the past, and confidently move forward toward achieving all of my dreams.

Journal

Use a journal to record your thoughts and answers. Practice CREATING the life you want to live. Dream big! After reviewing these questions, write out a narrative of what your life will be like in ten years.

Think about who you are right now.

- How do you feel?

- What are the things that make you happy in your life?

- What are the things that break you down?

- Is there any negativity in your life right now? Where does it come from?

- How do you handle stress? Do you have an outlet?

- How do you spend your time?

- What are your passions?

- What do you enjoy doing?

- What makes you laugh?

- What else defines you or brings your personality to life?

What can you let go of?

- Toxic people or a toxic environment?

- Your own inner voice that has a toxic thread to it?

- Previous experiences that have built up walls around who you really are?

Think about the life you want to lead ten years from now.

•◆ How would people describe you?

•◆ What is important to you?

•◆ Where do you live?

•◆ What do you do?

•◆ What is your home like?

•◆ Who is around you?

•◆ What is your day like?

Create your ten-year vision, timeline, and goals. (Refer to sample earlier in this chapter.)

Step 1: Write out a short vision statement, based on the narrative you created above. You should be able to state this in thirty seconds or less.

Step 2: Align incremental milestones to your vision of one year or longer.

Step 3: Create a set of smaller goals that will align with your vision and milestones.

GOAL-SETTING WORKSHEET

Current Date: _____

10-year Vision Statement

Milestones:

1 year

3 years

5 years

7 years

10 years (equals vision statement)

1 year goals—to reach milestone(s)

1 month

3 months

6 months

9 months

12 months (equals 1-year milestone)

- Put these goals in play by using a tracking system.

- Tell someone about these goals to make yourself accountable.

Create Your Own Canvas (optional)

Art

- List the goals for your one-year milestone (that align to your ten-year vision).

- Assign a color to each of them.

- Create a masterpiece assigning each word/goal a color and creatively adding each color to your canvas.

- Place your masterpiece in a place that reminds you of it daily.

House

- Clean, organize, paint, add an accent piece or color.

- Create a special place in your house for your "me-time" or meditation.

- Allow yourself to have peace and inspiration in your house.

Meditation

- Try cleansing your mind, heart, and soul through your deep breathing.

- Practice the meditation technique I provided in this chapter or one you have found that inspires you.

Miracle 4

Empower

Find happiness first.

The color of EMPOWER: Yellow

The scents of EMPOWER: Yuzu, Lemon, Verbena

Many believe that when a goal is reached,
happiness will arrive. But happiness isn't an outcome.
Happiness is what creates the outcome.

—JULIE

The secret to happiness—it's what we live for each day. It's what we seek in our jobs, our relationships, our personal conquests. It's what this book is about. It's what 99 percent of what our life is about . . . figuring out the secrets, EMPOWERING ourselves, and unlocking the Miracles to finding happiness.

Each of us defines our own version of happiness differently, but we all desire the same thing—to have happiness in our lives. The challenge is that we tend to seek the solutions we need to be happy.

I want to inspire you to think in the reverse order. Be happy, and you will find all of the solutions that you seek.

I work with many clients who repeatedly tell me how desperate they are to lose ten pounds, how much happier they will be when they have more money, or how life will begin when they meet their soul mate. They are thinking an action, an activity, or an outcome will create their happiness.

After working with many clients over the past twenty years, I can say, without hesitation, that this is the key to achieving anything:

Those who are successful choose to be happy first.

They choose to like who they are, what they are doing, and the possibilities of their future—right now. They find their joy within themselves without conditions. Yes, they have goals and aspirations, but they also know that the only thing for certain is this very moment. Therefore, they must embrace their feelings and actions in the present. They choose to be happy. They choose to find happiness despite the day, situation, or challenge. They know one of the secrets to the 7 Life Miracles is to be happy first, and everything else will fall into place.

Finding happiness first can be difficult. In a world where we are judged, rewarded, and accepted by our job, our physique, our looks, or our monetary status—it can be difficult NOT to let those things dictate our happiness. It is easy to let ten pounds break our confidence; it is easy to let our economic status indicate how well we are doing in society; it is easy to focus on the people who seemingly have everything we wish we had.

However, "things" do not bring happiness. In fact, some people who are the wealthiest, the thinnest, and the most beautiful are not happy. The reason? There is always someone wealthier, thinner, prettier, something-er. They are never "good enough" as they are— they are constantly trying to find happiness through their actions. Yet these actions do not create happiness. They are secondary to it. Happiness is intrinsic—it comes from within. Happiness is a choice.

Happiness is trusting that you are right where you are supposed to be, you have everything you need, and you will be okay no matter what happens. Happiness is waking up and smiling for no reason except that you are blessed with another day to live your life to the fullest. Happiness isn't something that is taught. It is something that you give yourself permission to be. It cannot be bought. It is free to those who want it.

Side note: I am not saying that wealthy people are unhappy. Those who are wealthy can be extremely happy if they are not dependent on material goods to satisfy their success. Material goods can be fun and provide great experiences, but only when you choose to be happy first. One of my closest friends is extremely successful in her life—financially, professionally, and personally. She radiates happiness. When asked the secret to her success, her response was, "Keep moving forward, be grateful for today, and cherish your family and friends."

Happiness Through a Child's Eyes

Many times our greatest lessons of the Miracles come from children. In a previous chapter I mentioned meeting Rory—a brave young man who ended up paying forward on the lessons in his life. I met Rory and Cody, the young man I am going to tell you about, because I am a volunteer wish granter for an organization that grants wishes for children with life-threatening illness. I have had the privilege of working with over thirty-five "wish" families over the past fifteen years and have been inspired by their strength, love, and compassion.

The following wish is one that changed my life and taught me the true meaning of happiness.

Cody

Cody was a beautiful nine-year-old boy—full of life, happiness, and laughter. Despite his being in a wheelchair because of his illness, I never really noticed the wheelchair. Cody's presence and love of life far outweighed any disability, sickness, or challenge he was facing. No matter how sick Cody was, he never once complained. He always smiled and said that his life was full of love.

I will never forget the first day I met him. He was racing around his house in his wheelchair, wearing a cowboy hat, competing against his cousin who was not in a wheelchair—and they were laughing. Have you ever watched kids play and found yourself smiling? There is a simple joy in their play that we adults tend to forget; Cody helped me find a little more joy in my life that day and each day since.

When the race was over, Cody caught his breath and came over to meet me. I introduced myself as his wish granter. We talked for a while, and I asked him about his life. Then came the big question: "If you had one wish, what would it be?"

He smiled and said, "I'm fortunate. I have friends and I have family and I have love. Those are the things you take with you for all time." He seemed like such a wise soul for one so young. I wondered if by chance Cody was an angel on earth—to be so mature, so patient with his illness, so loving. He was remarkable from the moment I met him.

He then named an actor that he wanted to meet. "He is my hero. He always wins in any battle he is up against, and he has taught me that you can be strong in any situation. He also shows me that good triumphs over evil. So, I want to meet him and ride horses with him."

Cody smiled and looked at me without any evidence of doubt that this could happen. This particular hero, I'll call him Connor, happened to be one of the most famous actors of our time and starred in action movies where he was always the good guy. As wish granters, we are taught to ask for a second wish, in case for some reason the first one can't be granted. This is especially true with celebrity wishes. While most celebrities are fabulous to work with, granting the wishes can take time, and these kids don't always have a lot of time to wait.

When I asked Cody about his second wish, his answer was, "I don't have a second wish. That's my wish. And I don't have a lot of time left, so you'd better just go ask him."

Fast-forward a year or so later. We received a call that Cody was becoming sicker. He had lost all strength in his lower body, he was unable to use his arms, and he was no longer able to give his famous "Cody hugs." When he wanted to hug someone, his mother would have to wrap his arms around the person and then he would tap his fingertips along their back and that was his version of a hug. (And it is one of the best hugs I have ever received.)

Within days, we also received a call that Cody's hero was going to arrange for Cody to come to his ranch to grant his wish. I took the information to Cody (limo ride to airport, flight, and the details of his adventure with Connor). I have never seen anyone grin as big as Cody grinned that day. I could feel the excitement radiating from his body.

When Cody and his family arrived at Connor's horse ranch on a weekday, Connor and his family were there to greet him. Wish granters don't usually travel, so I wasn't present at the wish, but I was later given a video of Cody's big day. They had lunch and then Cody indicated to Connor that he wanted to ride horses with him. This is where my heart dropped. I wondered, *How could this really happen? Cody is mostly paralyzed and extremely weak and frail.* Cody's hero became my hero as well when he didn't even pause or have to think twice; he got up on his horse, held Cody in his arms in front of him, and the two of them rode his horse.

I have been blessed to see many beautiful things in my life, but Cody riding the horse with Connor? It may have been the most beautiful thing I have ever witnessed. Cody's face lit up—almost as if he had an internal light radiating from him. What struck me so much about this is that Connor chose to see the possibilities in the request from Cody—not the limitations. He must know a thing or two about happiness.

Connor spent the rest of the time carrying Cody around the ranch, from barn to meadow to patio. Everywhere they went,

Connor carried Cody. That, too, was a beautiful thing. Connor let Cody sit on a horse saddle from one of his movies and even gave him a special sheriff's badge worn in one of his most famous movies. It was more precious than gold to Cody.

After Cody returned home, we got together to talk about the experience. I asked him what he thought of his wish. He answered, "It was the best day of my life. I felt as if I was fully alive. My hero carried me when I didn't have the strength to carry myself. Connor was even better in real life than he was in the movies. I will never forget him, the kindness he showed, and the strength he gave me. Thank you for making my wish come true."

I drove home that day crying that cry you have when you are overwhelmed with (good) emotion. I realized that Cody was indeed an angel on earth—and I felt blessed to have met this angel. While he believed that he had met his hero, Cody became the hero to all of us in his ability to find happiness.

A few weeks later, I received the news that Cody had passed. While I was extremely saddened, I also couldn't help but picture Cody in heaven, wearing his cowboy hat and badge, smiling and saying, "Friends and love are what you take with you for all time, and I have those things with me up here in heaven."

Yes, I wish I could have changed Cody's life and taken away his pain, suffering, and illness. But Cody's soul was wiser and stronger. He understood how to find the joy in his everyday life. He never thought of himself as unfortunate, and he never felt sorry for himself. He lived his life fully. He laughed every day. He affected the world in meaningful, powerful ways with his kindness, joy, and presence. Connor even blogged about how incredible Cody was; that Cody knew the secrets [or Miracles] to living—finding the joy within and not letting anything get in the way of that.

Be a Cody

Some days are going to be better than others, and some can seem unbearable. An illness, a death, the loss of a job, a breakup, a demotion, news you didn't want to hear . . . all of these things and plenty of others can break you down. Something challenging will come into your life no matter how happy you are . . . no matter how wealthy you are . . . no matter how healthy you are. Things happen, but what allows us to be happy in the face of these challenges is to trust that we have everything we need and that we can handle everything that crosses our path. At times God will place people (angels on earth), opportunities, or events in your way to help you along, but trust in the fact that you have everything you need. You don't need to worry about things. If you like the choices you make, if you like who you are when no one is looking—then you have everything you need. All you can be is your best, and to be your best, choose to be happy.

Where to Start?

So—what if you want to be happy and you understand everything written so far in this chapter, but you struggle with bringing this concept to life?

The quickest way to placing happiness in your life is by finding your gratitude. Gratitude is the simplest form of happiness; if you can find your gratitude in this moment, you can also find your happiness.

Practice finding your gratitude by focusing on one thing you are grateful for each night before you go to sleep and then thinking about one thing you are grateful for as you begin your day. Whatever energy surrounds you is the energy you will keep attracting to you. If you start your day by being grateful for your life, or at least one part of it, you will emit an energy field around you of happiness. Interestingly enough, the more you do this, the more all of your other dreams and goals begin to come true.

Start by finding gratitude. When you start there, you can't help but find happiness as well.

30-Day Happy Life Challenge

I do an exercise with clients who want to start working with me on a fitness/weight-loss goal. For the first thirty days, I don't place a large focus on physical training. Yep. You read it right. The reason is because of everything contained in this chapter. I need to know that their head is in the right place before we begin. I want them to find the joy in their lives right now. I want them to be open to the possibilities of their life. I want them to think about life elevation. Therefore, my clients go through a thirty-day self-experiment what I call "The 30-Day Happy Life Challenge."

I believe there are four key variables to being joyful and happy. We have to:

1. Be Inspired

2. Get Out of Our Comfort Zone

3. Continually Learn New Things

4. Take Time to Relax and Restore Our Body

For my 30-Day Happy Life Challenge, I have a list of hundreds of activities my clients can commit to that focus on each of those categories. For thirty days, they select one thing they will do every day to be Inspired, Dared, Coached, or Relaxed. They have to keep a running log of their adventures and what they learn throughout the Challenge. At the end of the thirty days, we sit down and talk about what they have done. It is remarkable to hear how much fun people have on their thirty days of challenge—and what a better mindset they are in to begin a fitness journey. They learn that everything we do is about an adventure—not a ritual. We do not do the same workout every day. We do not eat the same things every day. We are not robots—we are real, living, breathing, inspired people who need challenges, adventures, and fun to live out loud. Once they grasp this concept, the program I develop for them each week becomes more of an adventure than a painful commitment. When they find their own happiness first, I know they will be successful in anything they attempt.

I believe that you also can find happiness in thirty days or less. Try it out!

This chapter's Miracle is truly a life-changing one. Find happiness first. Give off positive energy. See the glass half full. Take a deep breath and smile when stuck in traffic. Trust that you have everything you need—right here, right now. Find gratitude in the moment. See the world as you wish it to be, and strangely enough, it will be.

UNLOCK MIRACLE #4 IN YOUR LIFE

MEDITATION

Today, I choose happiness first. I choose to start and end the day with gratitude. I choose to fill everything in-between with gratitude. Gratitude is the quickest way to place positive energy in the world, and whatever I give out is what I attract. Something I am grateful for at this moment is_____. I am blessed beyond measure. I have everything that I need to be successful. I have goals and aspirations that I am working toward, but I am joyful at this moment in time. I will look for ways to be inspired; I will get out of my comfort zone; I will learn something new; I will relax. I recognize that each of these elements helps me to be empowered, more resilient, and happier.

Journal

Use a journal to record your thoughts and answers. Practice EMPOWERING the life you want to live.

1. Try your own 30-Day Happy Life Challenge.

   a. Fill the next thirty days with something that is related to one of the four following concepts:
      •◆ Being inspired
      •◆ Getting out of your comfort zone
      •◆ Learning something new
      •◆ Taking time for you/relax/restore your body

   b. Keep a log of your adventures and reflect upon them at the end of your thirty days.

2. Find your gratitude each day and keep a Gratitude Journal.

   a. Write down one thing you are grateful for when you wake.

   b. Write down one thing you are grateful for when you go to sleep.

   c. Remember that whatever energy you surround yourself with will be the energy you give off to others and the energy you feel within.

Miracle 5

Choose

There is more than one path.

The color of CHOOSE: Green

The scents of CHOOSE:
Lemongrass, Green Apple

*There are choices in every moment or situation . . .
we are never stuck.*

—JULIE

Have you ever felt stuck in your life? Or perhaps stuck in a situation? Most of us have at one time or another, and when we feel stuck, we don't move forward. This chapter is focused on unsticking what may be stuck and moving forward in a direction that is powerful, positive, and inspiring. The Miracle in this chapter is a well-kept secret of people who are successful. Incredibly, this secret is quite simple.

The best way to prevent yourself from getting stuck in your life is to remember this basic truth:

***There are always choices available to you at every moment.
It is up to you to decide which you will CHOOSE.***

(Although there is an endless supply of choices to make in every moment, for simplicity's sake we will focus on the idea that you have at least two.)

Swings or Monkey Bars?

I am convinced that children understand the concept of "choice" far better than most adults. This is probably because it originates from simple ideas. The concept of "choice" comes from ideas that you may have known at one time or another, but due to the complexity and busy-ness of life, you may have forgotten them.

School children at recess who don't like the swings, play on the monkey bars. It's that simple. Kids don't get upset about the swings; they just move on to something else that they find is more fun. They don't talk about the swings. They don't mock the swings. They don't kick dirt at the swings. They just play on the monkey bars instead.

You too have the opportunity, every minute of your life, to choose whether you play on the swings or the monkey bars. It is often so easy to get fixated on the swings in life that the monkey bars aren't even considered. But if you can remember the simple idea that you have a choice in how you handle EVERYTHING in your life, then opportunities and Miracles start to show up everywhere.

Choices, Choices, Choices

In every moment, we have an opportunity to make choices that make us feel good and help us move toward our goals and personal commitments. In that same moment, we also have the choice to do something else.

- Go to the gym or sit on the couch.

- Eat grilled chicken or fried chicken (or grilled/fried tofu!).

- Call a friend and talk, or sit and think about being lonely.

- Be productive at work, or sit and stare at the computer.

There are times when it really can be that simple. Our life is in constant motion, and as we move, everything that we do is a choice. If you find yourself saying, "I wish I . . ." or "One day I will . . ." you just have to know that you CAN make another choice today. You CAN start your sentences by saying: "I am . . ." or "Today I will . . ."

You may be thinking, *It's not that simple. I have a busy life, and I don't have time to do these things I want to do.*

My response is very straightforward. You choose what you do. You choose where you spend your time. You choose your priorities. It may be difficult, and you may have to shift things around, but if you really want to do something, you can find a way to do it instead of doing what is getting in the way. You choose how you live your life.

- *Do what you want to do.*

OR

- *Do what gets in the way of what you want to do.*

Whether it is a *mindset shift* or a *directional change* in your life, everything is a choice: You decide how you feel, what you do, and who you are at every moment.

Choosing Your Mindset

My mother used to say to me, "Julie, life is up to interpretation. In this moment or in this situation, choose the interpretation that is the most powerful and positive for you. Choose what helps you to be your best." And she was right.

Anytime something didn't go the way I had hoped it would, I suffered from "analysis paralysis." I would obsess over what I did wrong, what I could have done better, and how I would do it differently in the future. Can you identify?

Missing your flight, a tough day at the office, or a bad decision . . . all of these matter, but they are rarely tragedies. They are things that you can learn from, make peace with, and move on. But when you hold on to these things and beat yourself up over them, the only thing you are doing is making yourself feel less powerful. You have the option to choose how you will handle each of the challenges that come into your life.

It isn't about the situation—it is how you choose to see it and what you choose to do with it. The following are some scenarios that tend to trip us up:

SITUATION	COMMON RESPONSE	POSITIVE MINDSET
Fitness program derail	Fitness just isn't for me. Every time I try, I fail.	That program wasn't right for me, but I am going to look into other programs that look fun and find a partner to keep me accountable.
Relationship breakup	I'll never meet anyone as wonderful ever again.	I am available to meet the right person. I will focus on taking care of myself so that when I meet that person, I feel confident in who I am.
Work error	I could get fired; I can't believe I did that.	I have learned a valuable lesson. I will make sure my boss knows what I learned and how I will handle this situation in the future.
Driving errors	I am stupid; I can't believe I missed my exit. Now I am going to be late.	Maybe there was an accident that I avoided. There is another exit just up ahead.
Money concerns	I don't know how I will pay all of my bills.	I will call my credit card company and ask them to put me on a payment plan. I will create a financial plan to understand how much I can spend each month. I will pick up additional work on the weekends to help pay down my bills.

Your mindset is a powerful everyday tool you can use to help you move forward. Go back and read each of the examples listed and think about the outcome in the Common Response column; then think about the outcome with a Positive Mindset. Do you notice how the Positive Mindset chooses to see opportunity and create a plan? Creating the plan is key to moving forward. You have to know what your next step is in order to take it.

Mindset: Baby Steps

Just by changing mindset, you can overcome hurdles, break down barriers, let go of the past, and move forward into the future. At first, practice using a positive mindset on the little things in your life. Get used to how it feels to look toward the positive side. Then start progressing to the bigger things. Because the truth is, it is okay to be angry, hurt, sad, disappointed, and any other emotion. But the more you teach yourself to turn the situation into the best possible outlook, the less weighed down you will feel. Those negative emotions usually do the reverse of your intentions. They only hold you back and keep you down. Choose to transition them into something that helps you move forward more quickly.

Mindset: Focus on What You Have

It's common to think about life in terms of what you used to have— perhaps comparing yourself to another time in your life when everything seemed to be going right. It's easy to make this comparison and then be depressed over it. I challenge you to choose a mindset that is focused on being grateful for what you have in your life right now. You always have these two choices—you can look back and compare, or you can march forward.

My parents divorced when I was four years old. A few years later, my mother remarried a man who became my dad. Growing up, my biological father was not present in my life.

For much of my childhood, I wondered why my biological father had left. I felt a sense of not being good enough and thought if I were a stellar student, athlete, and leader, perhaps he would take notice and want to come back into my life.

It wasn't until my freshman year in high school that I realized I had been choosing to see a negative interpretation of my life. I was at a track meet and lining up at the start, about to run my favorite event. I began my ritual of preparation: right foot in starter block, left foot in starter block, take three deep breaths, look up for my mom and dad in the stands, smile, look forward, and move as soon as I hear the gun go off.

As I looked up and caught the attention of my dad, it dawned on me that I already had something I'd been seeking my whole life. I wanted my dad, and there he was—at my track meets, my choir concerts, and through my boyfriend sagas. He was there for me and loved me as his only daughter. It didn't matter that I wasn't his biological daughter—we were a family, and he was my dad. Prior to that, I chose to think that my biological father had left. After that day, I realized that my dad had been with me all along. I chose to see the interpretation that was most powerful for me.

I am grateful that my dad is in my life. He has never left my side, and each year, we continue to be closer. He provides everything a daughter could need. I am blessed beyond measure.

(It is important to note that I do not have any negative energy toward my biological father. I understand he had to do what was best in his life. I think nothing but positive thoughts and wish him happiness. I have made peace with the things that bothered me in the past. I am blessed and grateful that he gave me life.)

Mindset: Big Deal Stuff

I was discussing this concept with a client of mine, and he said, "What about the big deal stuff, like losing a loved one? How do I keep a positive mindset about that? To me, that would be inauthentic to try to find the positive side of losing someone I loved."

This concept is not about always choosing to paint flowers and sing songs all day long. Sometimes there are big things that happen that are extremely painful and difficult. Losing someone close to you, experiencing a tragedy, being blindsided by something you never asked for or expected . . . these things are incredibly painful, and you have every right to take the time to feel what you need to feel without sugarcoating it or pretending it isn't difficult. There is always a natural healing process. You might experience sadness, fear, disappointment, loneliness, anger . . . and those feelings are all okay. It is up to you to decide when you can make peace with those feelings.

A friend of mine had cancer and passed away at the age of thirty-eight. She had a horrible journey the last two years of her life. Whenever she wrote to me, she was always hopeful that one day she would be healed from her cancer, and I could teach her yoga. I never expected her to pass. Quite the opposite. I had every intention of helping her with her comeback story through yoga and being a positive friend in her life. When I received the news that she had died, I was beside myself. I went through the stages of grief that most do—shock, sadness, anger, frustration. I asked myself if I could have been a better friend—if I could have comforted her more in her time of need. I spent an entire night crying over her passing, wondering if I could have done more, wishing I had. I cancelled a dinner I had planned with friends that night, letting them know I just needed time to myself.

One of them responded, "She'd be mad if she knew you were beating yourself up like this. All she would want you to do is keep sharing your love and inspiration with others, the way you shared it with her. And if you feel you have unfinished business with her, she can hear you, so just tell her what you need to say."

It was as if a weight had been lifted from my shoulders. My friend was right. I didn't have to make peace with cancer. I just had to make peace with myself and remember my friend as a gift in my life. I spent time writing her family and some close friends, sharing memories and posting photos of her. It helped us all. I prayed to her and told her I was sorry I never got to teach her yoga and I would do it when I got to Heaven.

Ironically, the next day, her sister (whom I have never met) emailed me and asked if I would teach her yoga. She knew that had been my plan for her sister. In some small way, I felt like that was my friend still giving me the chance to share my passion with her. I realized my prayer had been answered. My mindset had been changed. I was going to celebrate her life, not spend my time mourning her death.

I could have spent all of my time fixated on what a tragedy it was; that would be easy to do because it was, indeed, a great tragedy. But that doesn't help anyone—it simply delays healing. So my advice on the "big deal" stuff is to feel what you need to feel, as long as you need to feel it; make peace with yourself or the situation the best you can; and find a way to move forward, taking the things that are precious and good with you. Typically, that means to enlist your friends and family to get through it together.

Choosing Your Direction

Sometimes choice is about deciding your mindset—or how you will feel and react to a situation. Other times, choice is about consciously electing which direction you want to head in your life.

After I gave a lecture in Boston, one of the participants came up to me and explained he had heard me talk many times. He shared that this specific topic—Choose—was the one that had been the most powerful in his life. Miracles had happened in his life since he had adopted this concept into his daily routine:

"I always used 'time' as an excuse. I am a business executive. I travel all over the world. I have a lot of responsibility. I have a family. I never seemed to have enough time in my day to finish my job and take care of my family, let alone take care of myself. I heard you talk about choice and a light bulb went off. It took me about three months to organize myself to be able to do it, but I am now working out every morning before going to work, I've lost twenty pounds, I have more energy, and my family tells me I am a lot more fun to be around. My boss pulled me aside this week and asked me what I was doing differently, as he has noticed a positive change.

"I realized that I had to make the choice to unstick myself from the pattern I was in. All I had to do was take an hour out of the day for me and everything else in my life has gotten better! It was a choice to find the time. It wasn't easy, but I am so glad I did. Most people get stuck, feeling as if they can't find the time. But I am proof that it's a choice."

Everything is a choice. He changed the direction in his life by simply choosing to say, "I am doing it today!" vs. "I'll do that someday."

Direction: Tug at Your Heart

As you may recall from Miracle 2, I began my career right out of college in my dream job, working for my dream company. For the first few years of my career, I was extraordinarily happy and felt like, "This is it! This is my dream!"

But a few years later . . . something happened.

At the age of twenty-seven, I ran my first marathon. I ran it in Alaska. I went by myself. It was a very personal accomplishment. And it was a life-changing accomplishment. I had not only overcome the life expectancy predictions brought on by my heart, I had run a marathon—26.2 miles. No one in their wildest dreams would have imagined that I, the girl who was born with holes in her heart, would ever be able to run a marathon.

I flew home that week and thought about the marathon. I thought about how I was given a second chance at life. I thought about how my heart had healed because of healthy choices I had made in my life (and of course, because of God). I realized I had been given a gift in my life—to live. But a gift is only as good as what one does with it. I asked myself if I was using this gift in positive ways in my everyday life.

I heard myself answer, "No."

As weeks passed, I was restless. I kept thinking about my life, what my purpose was, where I was headed, what I was doing, and if I was happy.

Have you ever had one of these times in your life? It can be overwhelming. You have all of these thoughts in your head, but don't know what to do with them.

I sat down and wrote a note to God about it. I have always lived by the principle that when you make your intentions known, the world around you will cultivate an environment that will help you to succeed. In other words, "Put it into the world and doors will open."

Dear God,

I am grateful for all of the gifts and experiences in my life.

I love the company I work for, and I love the job I have been blessed to do. It has been a "dream job." It has been everything I asked for in a career, and everything I asked for in a company.

Despite this, I am feeling restless. After running that marathon in Alaska, I realized you have given me a second chance at life. You have healed my heart through health and wellness, and I think I am meant to share that story and inspire others to heal their own bodies. I feel a tug at my heart, as if you are asking me to use the gift of a second chance at life to impact others in a powerful way.

If I listen to what my heart is telling me, I think I am meant to take my passion for wellness and impact my colleagues by helping to start a corporate wellness program. In order to do that, I'll have to make some changes in my life. These changes are scary, new, and uncertain. Here are my concerns:

• I don't know much about this area outside of my own experiences, and so I'd have to go back to school and earn a Master's degree to achieve the proper credentials.

• I have a Bachelor's degree in International Business and so I won't be a prime candidate for any health or wellness degree program.

• I haven't saved any money to do this.

• I don't know if my company will start a wellness program, even if I get a Master's degree.

As you can see, I have a lot of unknowns. This feels very uncomfortable. I could just stay in my current job (which I enjoy) and not worry about things. But I feel like my LifeMap is telling me to change my path right now.

In order to take this leap, I need your help. For me to make this choice—to move my life in a different direction—I need to have a few things happen. If these things happen, I promise you, I will follow this tug at my heart and choose a different direction in my life.

Things That I Need to Happen:

• Get accepted into a Master's program at the school of my choice

• Receive financial support/scholarship

• Receive time away from my company to complete the program

• Have the security of returning to my company when the program is complete

Thanks for listening God, as always. I hope I am hearing you right and that I am moving in the direction you want me to . . . please just help me to know what to do.

I folded that piece of paper up, placed it in my laptop bag, and applied to take a graduate school exam.

Six Weeks Later

Rifling through my laptop bag, I found the letter I had written six weeks earlier. I opened it up and scanned down my list of "THINGS THAT I NEED TO HAPPEN." I was able to place a check mark next to each one of them.

• Get accepted into a Master's program at the school of my choice

- Receive financial support/scholarship

- Receive time away from my company to complete the program

- Have the security of returning to my company when the program is complete

Yes! All of those things happened! It was complete validation that I was on the right path. While it was still scary, I had the confidence I needed to move forward.

"Okay, God, I promised you. So, here goes!" I experienced the feeling of jumping off a ledge with my eyes closed, hoping there would be a soft landing below. There was . . . and much more.

I'll save the rest of this story until next chapter, but for now, I can say it was one of the best decisions of my life. Because of the choice I made, I was able to move my life in unbelievably powerful directions. I could have chosen to stay on the path I was on, and perhaps that would have gone well. But because I made the choice to listen to my heart and follow my passion and purpose, I now live my dream each and every day.

It's Your Choice!

When you are on the right path, everything around you helps you to be successful. Doors open where only walls stood before. It's when you dare to take the road that is uncomfortable, but filled with dreams and passions, that your greatest desires can be realized.

There are always (at least) two choices, two paths, two interpretations, in any moment, situation, or opportunity. This is true in both mindset and life direction. It is in recognizing this that passion, purpose, and joy are realized. Every moment offers a new choice. It is up to you to decide how you want to spend it. If you don't like a choice you made in the previous moment, simply make a new one right now. Remember, if you don't like the swings, simply choose the monkey bars.

UNLOCK MIRACLE #5 IN YOUR LIFE!

MEDITATION

I know that every day, every hour, every minute invites me to make choices. I do not have to continue to make the same decisions if they do not make me happy. It is up to me to determine how to make the choice that is the best for me. Sometimes I will play it safe and do what is best for my stability and comfort; other times, I will listen to that tug and accept the adventure my life has in store for me. I know that there will be times when I am not sure of the outcome, but I trust if I am following my passion and my purpose and I am trying to live with the intention of making the world a better place, the outcome will be magnificent. There are always two options in every decision, in every situation, in every moment. I will choose the ones that are the more powerful, inspiring, and positive for me and those around me.

Journal

Use a journal to record your thoughts and answers. Practice CHOOSING the life you want to live.

Mindset

Be aware of your choice of mindset. Pay attention to your feelings, thoughts, and reactions over the next few days.

1. Are there specific times that you tend to choose a path that limits you or holds you back?

2. Are there themes or people who tend to bring you down or cause you to focus on the negative?

3. Can you select one area of your life to focus on adopting a more positive mindset?

   •◆ How will you practice?

   •◆ What are some ways you can keep yourself from going down a negative path?

   •◆ Are there people whom you can use as positive influences to help you stay focused on moving forward?

Direction

Spend some time thinking about where you are headed based on your choices today:

1. Are you able to see the multiple options available to you?

2. Is there anything about your life that you feel is off track?

   •◆ Can you make a different choice?

3. What will your life be like if you choose to live within mediocrity?

4. What will your life be like if you choose to live your dreams?

   •◆ What small steps can you take to move your life in that direction?

5. Where will you find the courage to take that leap? (It usually isn't a big leap at first, but small steps that prepare you for the big leap.)

6. How will you remember that courage when times get tough?

Miracle 6

Climb

Conquer your mountains.

The color of CLIMB: Sky Blue

The scents of CLIMB: Fresh Mountain Air, Morning Dew, Rain

Nobody trips over mountains. It is the small pebble that causes you to stumble. Pass all the pebbles in your path and you will find you have crossed the mountain.

—AUTHOR UNKNOWN

"**Climb! Push! Stand up! Grit your teeth!** Use everything you have! Conquer this! Get to the top!" I passionately coach as the riders push their way up steep mountains.

When I teach an indoor cycling class, we hit a stage where the workout gets noticeably more difficult. I watch the riders as they grit their teeth, look focused, serious, and are no longer able to have a conversation. I know that at this point, when they have hit their edge or their true challenge, their minds and their bodies may encourage them to stop or slow down, but their hearts encourage them to push onward. I like to remind them, "The view is always best from the top because you have earned that view." I ask them to remember why they ride and what waits for them at the top of the mountain. Is it confidence, strength, endurance, the ability to overcome? What lesson will the mountain offer today?

You can translate the lesson from the cycling class into everyday life. It is easy to have a "good ride" when you are on a straight path that leads you to the finish line—but it is much more of a challenging and rewarding ride when you battle mountains, twists, and turns along the way that you didn't expect. Each of those mountains, twists, and turns teaches you something about your life and about yourself.

The Plan

Mountains are powerful and inspiring. They teach you how strong you are and how much you are willing to work to accomplish something. Mountains are also difficult. They appear unexpectedly, and they aren't typically part of "The Plan" that you envisioned for your life. They feel uncomfortable. Awkward. Uncertain. Frightening. Frustrating.

When you get frustrated by a mountain, it is for one of three reasons:

1. What's waiting for you at the top isn't what you really want.

2. You don't want it badly enough (yet).

3. You are learning how to conquer it.

It is important to recognize these reasons as you are battling the mountains in your life, because they can help you understand if you are heading in the direction that you desire.

1. **What's waiting for you at the top isn't what you really want.** Meaning: You are frustrated by your mountain because you

aren't motivated by the reward at the top. I had a client tell me consistently for several years that she wanted to do yoga. She would begin a yoga class, but never finish all of the sessions she bought. She would try again and again, but found the commitment to be too much of a challenge. Finally, we had a discussion about what her ultimate goal was, and she said it was to be more relaxed and calm. Her goal wasn't to do yoga; it was to be more relaxed and calm. We concluded that there are many other avenues she could take that would help her to achieve her goals. The reason she wasn't being successful was because she couldn't relax during yoga—rather, she felt more stressed because she didn't enjoy it. In other words, she was climbing a mountain that didn't motivate her. After our discussion, she put a plan in place to meditate/pray every day for five to ten minutes, perform a series of stretches several times a week at home, and treat herself to a massage once a month. This worked for her, and she feels much more relaxed and happy. She was able to commit to her plan because she enjoyed her journey and she wanted what waited for her at the top.

2. **You don't want it badly enough (yet).** Meaning: Whatever goal you are focused on attaining isn't as high a priority as the things that get in its way. For example, if you want to go to the gym four nights a week after work, but you are continually distracted by friends or family who want to meet for dinner, it means that your desire to go out to dinner is higher at this moment than your desire to be in the gym. Some of you may be thinking, *Of course! Who wouldn't want to do that?* And my response is, "Someone who feels that their health is the priority." You can always meet with friends or family after the gym or invite them along. But if you constantly choose meeting up for dinner instead of going to the gym, you can conclude at this moment in your life that your priority is the choice you make most often. In order to make that other choice more important, it has to become more important than the things that get in its way.

3. **You are learning how to conquer it.** Meaning: You are on the right path, but lessons don't usually come quickly or easily. We sometimes have to climb the same mountain several times to figure it out. For example, if we find that we continually repeat the same challenge, we didn't quite learn the mastery skill of conquering it in the previous experience. Perhaps you always tend to date the same type of person. You don't mean to, but you realize time and time again that you are attracted to the same type of person, with the same characteristics that don't work in your life. You must step back and examine the truth of that situation. I can identify with this. I dated some amazing men, but they were all wrong for me. My friends would laugh at me each time I started to date someone new because he was the same type of guy as the one before! I realized that while I was attracted to certain things in a person, those things didn't work for me as my soul mate. I took a good look at what wasn't working and found that I needed to be open to meeting people who had qualities that worked well with mine. Sometimes we're lucky, and these lessons can come after just one or two failed attempts. But sometimes we keep repeating the same pattern until we finally realize what is happening.

Regardless of the challenge(s) you face, mountains don't pop up along your LifeMap coincidentally. Mountains are teachers that unlock the Miracles of your life. Every single time you are confronted with a challenge, a difficult situation, a journey with twists and turns and ups and downs, you can rest assured that this mountain was placed along your LifeMap to help you learn something.

Some of My Mountains

I started to recount one of my mountains—one that I am still climbing—in the last chapter. I made the choice to change the course of my life and to re-center myself to my LifeMap. That required my being open to an unfamiliar path and unchartered territory. At the end of the previous chapter, all of the "impossible" things on my list had happened in a matter of weeks. I considered it validation that this journey was indeed the path I was supposed to be taking. I was ready to start the next chapter of my life and get the education I needed to move in a new and powerful direction. But it didn't come easy. Here are just some of the mountains I faced on my path to changing my career and my focus. I have named each mountain, hoping that it will help you connect it to your own series of mountains.

Mountain #1: Being Humbled

Getting into graduate school was one thing, but actually leaving my job, becoming a student again, and making significantly less money to support myself was challenging.

My undergraduate work was in an entirely different field. In graduate school, I felt like I studied twice as hard for half the grade as everyone else. Some days I remember thinking, *I gave up a good-paying job to go back to school, study day and night, and barely get by with my grades. Was this really a smart decision?*

I was humbled, disappointed, and frustrated, and I questioned myself and my choice to go back to school. But of course, overcoming the struggle was exactly what I needed to learn the most.

> LESSON: It is the struggle that makes us stronger. Learning to overcome challenges is a lesson that will help me for the rest of my life.

Mountain #2: Stumbling Over the Obvious

While in graduate school, aside from dreaming of creating a corporate wellness program, I also wanted to develop my own personal business and create fitness videos, books, and be a lecturer and presenter. I felt that I had a positive message to share with the world, and I wanted to share it as wide and loud as I could! My first goal was to create a fitness video so I could reach a large number of people with my message. But creating a fitness video was not a small investment, and going back to graduate school had put a dent in my savings. I dreamed up other ways that I could get my goal off the ground.

I was a big fan of a popular daytime talk show host and loved how she helped real people make their dreams come true. I especially enjoyed how she highlighted people who were doing kind things in the world. I wondered, if she learned of my story, would she think I was worthy of helping?

I knew that she received thousands of emails every day, so if I were going to reach her, I would have to stand out (in a good way). So I wrote a letter about myself in third person, asking her to help get my inspirational messages out into the world. I sent this letter to 5,000 of my closest friends (anyone who was in my address book). I asked them to send that letter to a specified email address (the show's production manager), at a specific time, on a specific day. I figured that her staff may not see it if I send the letter in, but if thousands of people send the letter at the same time, on the same day, they would have to see it!

When that day came, I had over one thousand people copy me on their email notes, indicating their request for this host to help me launch my message and help me create my first fitness video. I was so excited! The possibilities were endless! I couldn't wait to receive her call.

The clock ticked. The minutes ran into hours. I waited a few days. A few weeks. And then after a few months, I realized that perhaps my plan had not worked. I felt disappointed, and I spent a lot of time thinking about what went wrong.

Then I realized that nothing went wrong. Everything went perfectly right! I was shown that there were over one thousand people who believed in me strongly enough to send a letter to an international superstar and ask her to support my effort.

THAT realization was more powerful than actually hearing back from the television host. It was at that moment I asked myself, *Why would she take a chance on me if I haven't taken a chance on myself? I have taken very little risk on this endeavor, and I was asking for help before I even tried to help myself. I need to take a chance on myself and in doing this, I will show that I am worthy for others to take a chance on me as well!*

With confidence that I could do this, I took on teaching seventeen fitness classes a week while in graduate school (not recommended and not safe—do not try at home!) so that I could earn the money to create my first fitness video. Once I had the money saved, I interviewed eleven media companies around my city, negotiated the best possible rate, and created my first fitness video. It was one of the best experiences of my life. (As a side note, the fitness students that I asked to star in this video with me turned out to become some of my best friends. More on them later.)

If we want to be successful at something, we have to go out and do the thing that will give us the success we're looking for. We cannot wait around for someone to pick us up; we cannot depend on someone else to take us under his or her wing. It is up to us to take that step, to believe in ourselves, and to put ourselves out there.

> **LESSON:** If you don't take a chance on yourself, no one else will either. This lesson of personal empowerment is something that will help me the rest of my life.

Mountain #3: Unplanned Bumps

Shortly after I released my fitness video, *Core Results*, I received a phone call from a sports agent. He said that he had seen my video and wanted to pick me up as one of his talent professionals. He said he only took a chance on one new person every year, but he liked my style and thought I could be the next "It" girl. He told me I would need to come to a weekend industry event in a certain large city, and if I could get there, he would turn me into a success. I would meet all the right people, and this would be the opportunity of a lifetime. He told me exactly what I needed to bring (product inventory, my computer for business transactions, my video camera, my regular camera, several new fitness outfits, several suits, and my best jewelry for attending dinners with prospective business executives). He said, "You want to dress to impress!" I checked him out on the Web, and it looked like he represented some great sports figures. I was honored and excited about this opportunity.

I took a flight to the city he mentioned with everything he told me to bring. I rented a car and parked at the convention center as he'd instructed me. I went into the center to find the event. I saw signs for the event, and I followed the arrows. I walked in and . . . it was empty.

There was no event. Someone had taken great measures to lure people to a specific location. I went back to my car and—sure enough—in the few minutes I was inside, it had been broken into and everything was stolen. I went to security and the security officer said, "You parked in the one location in the garage that the cameras don't see." Guess who told me to park there.

I lost everything I had that helped me with my business. Everything.

After flying home (bagless) and having a freak-out session for a few days, I put myself back together and created a new plan. My business dreams would be delayed for a bit, as I had lost a great deal of material goods, but I created a plan that would allow me to earn them back and get on track again. And I did.

> LESSON: People can take away everything you own, but they can never rob you of your passion. Learning I am more valuable than my possessions is another lesson that will help me for the rest of my life.

Mountain #4: Kicked While Down

Remaining positive, I focused on my plan to get back on track. Thinking about it now, I cannot comprehend how I went to graduate school full time, was a graduate assistant for 10–15 hours a week, and worked an additional 20+ hours a week teaching fitness classes and conducting fitness tests. In addition, any extra time I had was spent applying to any health and wellness magazine that would feature me and list my fitness video at no charge to me.

There is no one more passionate than a person who has stumbled and wants to get back up. I had a fire in my soul to turn my past challenges into successes and follow the trail laid out on my LifeMap!

One day, I received a letter from a woman who let me know she had seen my video in a magazine that she subscribed to. She said that she had bought the trademark rights to my company name and that I was illegally using it on my video. She gave me thirty days to pull all of my videos off the shelves, out of distribution, and rebrand with a new name or she would press charges.

At first, I thought this was an error, as I had trademarked my company name nationally. Unfortunately, I learned that there was an oversight in the trademark database, and while I owned the name nationally, she owned it in her city, and I could not promote any of my products in any magazines that could reach anyone in her city.

I called an attorney, and he quoted me more than ten thousand dollars to go to court over it. I called my production company, and they quoted me significantly less to edit the video by removing the name and rebranding with a new name. I pulled my product from the shelves, rebranded the video with a new name, and started over again.

But—I still had a great video, I still had my passion, and I looked forward to what the years to come would bring.

> **LESSON:** It is important to know when you can be flexible and when you have to stand strong. I could be flexible with my company name, but stood strong on the fact that I would still keep moving forward with my business. Learning to be flexible is another lesson that will help me for the rest of my life.

Mountain #5: Closed Doors

At this point, I had to get resourceful. Because I had hoped the video would be a springboard to launching other videos, books, and lectures, I had to get creative. I had to look for other ways to get my video in front of the right people.

Someone mentioned that the home-shopping television channels might be a good way to go. I could have my product in front of millions of people, and even if I didn't make much off the deal, I would get national exposure that could open up possibilities.

I applied to have my fitness video featured on one of the home-shopping channels and received an invitation to come to New York City to pitch my product for fifteen minutes to a potential buyer. I researched this offer very carefully! And—unlike my other trip—this was the real deal. The address checked out, and the name of the contact checked out. I worked overtime for three weeks, bought a plane ticket to NYC, and took a day off from graduate school. I had a fifteen-minute appointment scheduled for three o'clock in the afternoon. I would land at La Guardia at 11 a.m., take a cab to the location, and practice my elevator pitch until 3 p.m., give the pitch, get back in a cab by 5 p.m., and catch a 7 p.m. flight home.

Everything was going as planned. I arrived on time and took a cab to the address on my invitation. When I got out of the cab, I saw a line of people that went down two New York City blocks. I thought to myself, *Whatever that line is for, I'm glad I don't have to wait in it!* I walked up the stairs to go into the lobby and a security guard stopped me. I explained that I had a three o'clock appointment, and he laughed. "So do all of those people."

I looked down the long line of people and realized that my appointment wasn't a special time for me. Rather, it was the time they gave anyone who had written the channel to pitch a product. I walked the two New York City blocks to stand at the end of the line.

I could fill pages of this book with all of the crazy contraptions and inventions I saw that day. At times, they made the wait better; other times, much worse. It took me two and a half hours to get through the line and into a room of 100 people. Each of us had four minutes to pitch an idea to a buyer, then a buzzer would go off and we were ushered out for the next group. When the start buzzer rang, my buyer walked up to me, and said, "You have four minutes. Tell me why your product needs to be on our channel."

I began my well-practiced elevator spiel. Within thirty seconds, she stopped me. "Are you selling a fitness video?" I said that I was. She apologized and let me know they would not be accepting any fitness videos through this process. She said I would have to send it in, have it reviewed, and if they liked it, I would have to agree to sell it for at least 50% of what I sold it for on my website. She wished me luck and walked away. I still had three minutes remaining on the timer.

In shock, I left the audition hall. I walked past a woman who was selling pet rock clothing, and then turned the corner to see a man with a sock puppet soap dispenser. I walked out of the building and felt one tear hit my cheek. I quickly hailed a cab to the airport, checked in, and was soon on my way back home.

No matter how resilient, strong, and positive a person I thought I was, this felt as though I were plunging off a mountain and could do nothing to break my fall. Every attempt I had made to get my message and my video out to the public had failed. I was doing all of this to help people. I didn't know why it seemed as if I were being held back in every way. I had been robbed; I had worked excessive overtime so that I could buy two plane tickets to places that turned out to be dead ends; I had been threatened with a lawsuit and had to rebrand my entire company and video. It seemed that nothing was on my side, and I felt like a failure.

I got home and thought about this journey. Was God trying to tell me this was the wrong direction? Or was He showing me just how much I believed in this? Ironically, the more difficult the journey became, the hungrier I got to share my positive message with the world. It was almost as if the mountains in my life increased my desire to succeed. Or maybe they just taught me that I could.

Bound and determined, I did the only thing I could think of to do without a lot of money, but with a lot of passion and belief. I posted a five-minute demo of my fitness video to YouTube. It was a free service, which was all I could afford. I then went about my life trying to refocus and rebuild my bank account.

Four months later, as I was graduating from graduate school, without promotion or pitching, my video sales skyrocketed. I was receiving international orders—I had people in countries around the world asking me if they could buy my videos and resell them in their shops! I began receiving phone calls to present fitness concepts at national and international shows.

Do I need to say this was a game-changer for me?

It took losing everything I had (except my passion) to discover what I needed to do—and it had been at my fingertips the entire time. The success I was seeking was already within me. I just had to look past the roadblocks to see the simple solution, and then use the tools that were available to me.

> LESSON: Sometimes the answers are right in front of us, but we spend so much time looking for them in other places, we miss that they were there all the time. We have to be able to bounce back from any fall and see the door that is open to us. This lesson of resiliency is something that will help me the rest of my life.

Mountain #6: Blind Faith

When I received my Master's degree, I felt like I had learned a lot. I had learned how to be a student again. I had learned in-depth textbook knowledge about exercise physiology and had real-world experience through the clinicals that were a part of the program. My professors were inspiring, brilliant, and excited for me and my journey. They taught me about myself and about the possibilities that were before me. On the days I wanted to give up, they reminded me why I shouldn't. They were coaches in my life, and I will never be able to pay them back for the gifts they gave me.

Through all of my lessons in graduate school, perhaps my greatest lesson was to be able to keep moving forward—despite the mountains that got in my way. I took that lesson with me as I returned to my former company.

When talking with Human Resources about returning, I was encouraged to come back into a regular position and see if I could eventually sell my idea of wellness to leadership. I agreed. I was happy to return and excited about being given an opportunity that had the possibility of bringing my dream to life.

From the moment I dreamed of doing this, it took me seven years to have my wellness concept officially approved. I believed in what I wanted to do, so I began developing several grassroots wellness efforts that cost me nothing and were organized during my non-work hours. These efforts grew, catching the attention of leadership, and eventually opened the door to a position that oversees an international wellness program for over 40,000 people. My dream come true!

> **LESSON:** If you believe it, it is possible. It may not happen overnight, but it will happen. Learning to trust myself is another lesson that will help me for the rest of my life.

I have so many stories of getting sidetracked, flipped upside down, turning right instead of left, and hitting my mountains along the way. I wanted to highlight a few to remind you that everyone has mountains. They will come in different shapes and sizes, and at different points and times in your life. It is easy to see them as bad luck or something that makes you wonder, *Why is this happening to me?* I want you to remember that your mountains are not bad luck or a punishment. Your mountains are there to help you—your mountains are there to serve as teachers along your LifeMap. They will enable you to gain the wisdom, experience, and strength you need to live the life your soul intended.

It is common to let mountains get in the way, slow you down, and even deter you from the direction you were headed. That may be because the mountains are asking you to consider if the direction you are heading is what you really want. It is okay if you decide it isn't, and it is okay if you decide it is. The mountains are not judgmental, and they are only there to help you clarify your life. It is just as important to determine which mountains you don't want to climb as it is to determine the ones you do.

Keep in mind that you are never alone. Never. Even (especially) during the most treacherous climbs, the ones you have no idea how you will make your way up—you are never alone. Your guides and angels are with you all the way along your mountain climb. Ask them for help. Ask them for direction. Discuss the terrain with them. Let them know how you feel and what you need in order to continue your climb. They will see to it that you find the strength, energy, and path needed to make it to the top. They know your LifeMap and want you to succeed. They also know that the mountains in your life are a part of your LifeMap. Your guides and angels will make sure that you find hope—even when hitting the steepest part of the climb.

Why God Sends Us Best Friends

When left alone, your mind might talk you into quitting. That little voice in your head might tell you things are impossible, but your guides and angels will always whisper encouragement, wisdom, and possibility—if you choose to hear it. God sends all the tools, maps, people, guides, and keys we need to unlock the Miracles in our lives. Our job is to make sure our minds are open to receive them. If we aren't open, they just pass us by and we miss opportunities to live with greater joy and happiness.

During the timeframe of writing this book, I was faced with quite a few mountains. While I was excited for the journey, there were days when I was overwhelmed.

One day I had been challenged "to my max" and was experiencing many unexpected twists and turns. I walked to my mailbox and there among bills, junk mail, and magazines, I saw two brightly colored envelopes. They were from my best friend, Gina. Forgetting about all of the other mail, I immediately opened the first envelope to find a bright pink card with two women on the cover. There was a funny joke on the outside, and on the inside Gina had written about how grateful she was for our friendship. As I opened the second card, one with bright yellow flowers on it, I read the words, "I am so excited for all of the amazing things happening in your life, and I am with you every step of the way! One day you will look back and laugh at all of the struggles (and I will be laughing with you!). You are smart, brilliant, beautiful, and amazing, and you can do anything! It will all work out!"

As I walked back inside, I found myself beaming from ear to ear. I was overjoyed that she had taken the time to send me those positive cards. Sure, my mountains and challenges were still the same, but her energy and friendship helped me remember that I was blessed and fortunate; that among many difficult challenges, I also had many wonderful adventures. She reminded me that I had all of the strength I needed to climb my mountains with excitement, confidence, and happiness—and this is just one small example of the thousands of ways her friendship has helped me in my life.

God sent me an angel-in-human-clothing to remind me how to be strong on a day I felt weak. The same is true with you. Look for the people and things that appear in your life each day; they will help you to triumphantly march up your mountain.

Climbing Your Mountains with Confidence!

The next time you feel that you are approaching a mountain . . . or maybe you run into one when you aren't paying attention—remember the following seven tips. These tips will help you climb with confidence, strength, and endurance. You may notice some of these tips are related to other Miracles mentioned in this book—this is because all Miracles are connected to each other.

1. **Find your gratitude.** Gratitude is the quickest way to infuse your life with positive energy. No matter what mountains, twists, or turns your path brings, make sure to note one thing that you are grateful for each day.

2. **Determine your continuum of possibility.** Consider any situation you are dealing with. Think of the worst possible outcome of that situation and how you would handle it; then, think of the best possible outcome of that situation and how you would handle it. Chances are, the situation will fall somewhere in the middle of the best and worst outcome. You have already worked out how you can handle those extremes, so be confident and know that you can handle anything in-between.

3. **Develop your favorite breathing techniques to manage acute and chronic stress.** Breath is a life force. Often, when we are stressed or anxious, our body tends to change our breathing habits—sometimes our breath speeds up, and sometimes it slows way down. Find a breathing technique that allows you to control your breath and use it when you are confronted by challenging feelings, people, or events.

    A simple technique that I use is to take two breaths in, hold for a few seconds, and then slowly release in a long, calm exhalation. Repeat several times.

4. **Look and listen for your angels and guides.** Wouldn't it be nice to think you had a guardian angel with you, whispering the secrets to the universe in your ear at all times? You do. You have to start paying attention to the tugs at your heart, the repeating messages in your life, and the supposed coincidences (which aren't really coincidences at all) around you.

5. **Determine your boundaries.** It is easy to lose sight of who you are and what is important to you when going through a challenging time—so it is important for you to define those things upfront. Describe your life purpose in one sentence. Understand what the must-haves and the nice-to-haves are in your life.

6. **Praise yourself each day.** Go ahead—look in the mirror. Like what you see. Find the good that you do each day and recognize it in yourself. You might start by identifying small things, but

you'll eventually see you have become exactly the person you wanted to be. Perhaps you can start by simply praising yourself for the amazing person you are. Every time you walk past a mirror, stop, look at yourself, smile, and say, "You are amazing!"

Don't worry if this is hard for you. Know that you aren't alone. It will take time and consistent practice. We are our own worst critic, and it is easy to be disappointed in ourselves for one failure, but difficult to be proud of ourselves for one hundred successes. This has a domino effect. When we focus on the things that didn't happen as we had hoped, this becomes a habit and we lose our confidence and courage. We manifest a negative mindset that creates a cycle of constant disappointment and frustration. However, the concepts in this book are focused on creating a habit of seeing the good in your life and moving forward. It serves no good purpose to hold on to things that don't help you to be amazing.

7. **Create a habit of possibility.** How you see the world is a habit. You choose a habit of either seeing the glass half full or half empty. Practice using the half-full reaction to all of life's circumstances. Catch yourself when you react negatively or are hard on yourself. Find the possibility in each moment and situation.

Celebrate the Top!

When you come to a peak or mountaintop along the way, stop for a minute and enjoy the view. Remember that the mountain was there to teach you the lessons of life that your soul was born to learn . . . to remind you of how strong you are . . . to help you celebrate the amazing view once you reach the top. There will always be another mountaintop to conquer, so be sure to celebrate your victories along the way.

UNLOCK MIRACLE #6 IN YOUR LIFE!

MEDITATION

I CLIMB. I put one foot in front of the other, and I climb. The mountains in my life may be small or big, but I climb them all with the same commitment—to conquer them. I recognize that mountains are not punishment, but rather teachers. They teach me what I need to know—about the world, about others, and about myself. I am confronted by mountains to become stronger, wiser, and more confident each day. There will be days that the mountains seem too big, and I don't know where to begin. On those days, I will take a few deep breaths, I will look up, and I will put one foot in front of the other and begin my way up the mountain. There are no short-cuts; there is just my path and my climb to the top. On the toughest steps and steepest gradients, I will remember that I am learning something, and I will be patient with myself. I will open my mind to possibilities, and I will focus on learning from my mountains. Mountains aren't there just to be looked at; they are there for me to gain strength and courage, and they are there to be conquered.

Journal

Use a journal to record your thoughts and answers. Practice CLIMBING the life you want to live.

Spend some time thinking about the mountains you have faced in your life and what lessons you have learned from them. They could be little mountains or big mountains. Pick one. Spend some time thinking about it and understanding what the lesson was in that mountain. This exercise is not intended to bring up old difficulties, but to show you how your challenges have given you great strength.

- How did you handle it?

- What did you learn while going through it?

- What lessons did you take with you?

- How can you use that lesson as you move forward in your life?

The next time you face a mountain in your life, remember to use the following seven tools to help you conquer it. But don't wait for a challenge in your life to try these out. Practice these habits in your everyday living. What we practice in our everyday living is what we turn to when we are challenged. Make these habits in your life. Perhaps you start with one and focus on doing it every day. Once that becomes a habit (something you no longer have to think about to perform), move on to the next. Let the following seven concepts help you climb your mountains and enjoy the view from the top.

REVIEW

Seven concepts to help you climb your mountains and enjoy the view from the top:

1. Find your gratitude.

2. Determine your continuum of possibility.

3. Develop your favorite breathing techniques to manage acute and chronic stress.

4. Look and listen for your angels and guides.

5. Determine your boundaries.

6. Praise yourself each day.

7. Create a habit of possibility.

Miracle 7

Inspire

Be a light in the darkness.

The color of INSPIRE: Purple

The scents of INSPIRE: Blackberry,
Blueberry, Bergamot

People may not remember exactly what you did or said,
but they will always remember how you made them feel.

—AUTHOR UNKNOWN

A **wise woman who was traveling** in the mountains
found a precious stone in a stream. The next day she met
another traveler who was hungry, and the wise woman opened
her bag to share her food. The hungry traveler saw the precious stone and asked the woman to give it to him. She did
so without hesitation. The traveler left, rejoicing in his good
fortune. He knew the stone was worth enough to give him
security for a lifetime. But a few days later he came back to
return the stone to the wise woman.

"I've been thinking," he said. "I know how valuable the
stone is, but I give it back in the hope that you can give me

something even more precious. Give me what you have within you that enabled you to give me the stone."

—Author Unknown

Now, more than ever, the world needs us to give off light. It is too easy to spread darkness. Gossip, putting others down, cutting people off, speaking unkindly, not listening to others . . . sometimes these things are habits that form not because we want to be mean or thoughtless, but because they are easy defaults. When we are short on time, it is easier to make those choices.

But this Miracle challenges you to take the time to discover ways in which you can be a Light instead. In fact, I'll be so bold as to ask you to become a Light Warrior with me. I know that may sound silly, but bear with me; it's important. Being a Light Warrior has two parts: bringing inspiration to yourself and bringing inspiration to those around you. If that sounds good to you, and you accept the title "Light Warrior," your next step is to read on.

Inspire Yourself

I belonged to a church youth group when I was in high school, and this group had a profound impact on who I am today. The impact came from the people who led the group, as well as from the teachings. What I appreciated most about it was that we had fun—and while having fun, we learned how to be good people. Some of the most memorable moments of my teenage years came from being a part of this group. Maybe it was because it gave me a sense of belonging. Perhaps it was because the people who led the group believed in me and made me feel that I was someone special. Maybe it was because my very best friend in the whole world was in the group too, and since we lived in different cities, it was an opportunity to see each other each week. Or perhaps it was just that I had fun and was inspired each time I went. I'm guessing it was a combination of all of those things.

I remember the camping trips we took and how I loved being close to nature. My best friend Lisa and I would sneak away from the rest of the pack and make our own hiking trail. We would sit on some rocks, watch the stream flow by, and talk for hours. We took cassette tapes we had made of our favorite love songs, shared a headset, and sang along with the songs. We talked about meeting the man of our dreams one day and finding true love. We giggled as we described who we thought that man would be and how we would know he was the one. We picked up nearby stones and threw them in the stream, making wishes on them. Sometimes, instead of wishes, we would dedicate a stone-throw to our forever friendship or to happiness or to whatever we had been talking about, and then we each threw a stone in at the same time. We could spend a whole day doing this—without ever getting bored.

At night, we laid our sleeping bags next to each other so we could again share an earphone set and listen to music as we fell asleep. We loved music, we loved spending time together, and we loved enjoying the simple things. We had found joy without spending a lot of money, without a popularity contest, without a fancy car. We just enjoyed our time together. People often asked us why we were always smiling and happy. It didn't dawn on us until later in life that this was unusual. We just thought people were happy—as we had found a way to be happy and find the joy in each day. We knew that spending time together made us happy, so we chose to do that as often as possible.

That is the first half of being a Light Warrior. It is about taking care of you and finding happiness and inspiration each and every day. It is about making choices that allow your soul to radiate.

Personal joy, happiness, and inspiration are essential ingredients to living every day. If we cannot find these things each day, we didn't look hard enough. No matter what the circumstance, we can always find something that makes us feel inspired. The things that bring us our greatest joys and spark our happiness are personal, internally focused, heartfelt activities. Here are some ideas that might appeal to you:

- Listen to music.

- Spend time with a friend.

- Notice something you hadn't noticed before.

- Enjoy being with yourself; read a book, enjoy a sunset, write in your journal, enjoy a walk.

- Make extra time to be with your kids and/or family.

- Plant some flowers or a tree (and water them!).

- Play like a kid.

- Laugh with a friend (or by yourself).

These are all soul-nurturing activities. No matter what is happening in your life, if you can find the time to do one of these things, you can elevate your soul. Sometimes, that is all we need to do to change the course of our day, week, or life.

These ideas may seem easy on paper, but may be much more challenging when you're having a difficult day or week. But it is in those times that it is especially important to radiate light and inspiration. You can change your entire energy simply by finding something to be happy about.

Inspire Others

In our youth group, we had lessons on Sunday nights. Typically they were about a relevant topic to teenagers, but had a tie-in back to scripture. We sang, we played, we socialized, we ate, we volunteered, we camped, and we learned. On one particular Sunday night, our youth group leader brought in a special guest. Kelly worked with an organization that helped kids to find direction in their life. She talked to us about the kids she worked with—some were runaways; some hadn't eaten for days; some had to drop out of school to work because they had to take care of the family. I remember feeling overwhelmed by her stories. I couldn't imagine being in those situations. Although my family went through some tough times, we always had a meal to eat and a roof over our heads. We didn't always live in the fanciest places or have the most luxurious things, but we had enough—we had what we needed. And we were happy.

It was hard for me to fathom that there were kids like me, some even younger, who were facing so much responsibility and struggle. Despite the tough lives these kids faced, Kelly told us they didn't consider themselves down and out; they were just working through their needs. She said they still laughed, had friends, and enjoyed life—just like everyone else. One of the goals of her job was to teach them how to find the joy within themselves and to respect and appreciate others. By being able to do that, no matter what circumstance they faced, they would be able to come out on top. Again, I remember feeling shocked and stunned by the idea that these kids, who were struggling to make it day to day, could find joy within themselves and take the time to appreciate the joy in others. She had us do an exercise to learn the same lessons she taught them.

She gave us each a sheet of paper that had a drawing of a candle on it. She asked us to have someone tape this piece of paper to our backs. She then gave us each a marker and dimmed the lights.

"Find the Light in the Darkness," she said. We looked at her, a little surprised. "Go on. Find the Light in the Darkness. Life isn't always going to be bright and sunny every day—but you can always find a Light in the Darkness if you choose to. Walk around and find the candle on each person's back. Use your marker to write something that you appreciate about that person on their piece of paper. Create a Light in the Darkness for them."

At first we felt awkward, giggling and walking around in circles, staring at the clean sheets of paper on each person's back—until one person wrote on another person's paper, and all of a sudden everyone seemed to be writing on everyone else's back. We spent thirty minutes or so doing this exercise, with about forty teenage kids.

When we were finished, she asked us to remove the paper from our backs and read what was written on it. As we began to read what others had said, you could hear the laughter, happiness, and fun people were having. Some remarked, "I didn't know people thought that about me!" Others said, "Wow! This is really cool." I realized that sometimes we don't always tell people everything we should. Why had it taken an exercise in the dark to allow us to tell each other just how much we appreciated each other?

I walked to a corner of the room and read mine. I was surprised to see such positive things written. I guess I felt that my peer group thought I was an okay person, but I never really heard what people appreciated in me. I realized how powerful it was to help someone else to find a little joy in his or her life and feel valuable, liked and appreciated. That day changed my life. That day began my understanding of the 7th Life Miracle. That day has allowed me to understand my life purpose. More than twenty-five years later, I still have my Light in the Darkness paper.

As we were quieting down from reading our papers, Kelly gathered us back together and said, "This exercise wasn't really an exercise. You have the choice to do this every minute of every day of your life. It's about seeing the positive—even in the toughest times. It's about finding the good things in each person, no matter what the situation is. It is about bringing joy, recognition, and happiness to another person. And we have that choice right now. You can choose to use this moment as an opportunity to see the Light in someone, or you can choose to see the Darkness."

She went on to say, "When you are walking down the street and you see someone who is different from you—perhaps their socio-economic status is different, their clothing choice is different, or even the way they carry themselves is different . . . it is common for us to say something, even if out of earshot of the other person, that belittles them. It may not be intentional—it may be something that we say that puts someone else down so we can feel better about ourselves, but I encourage you to catch yourself as you do this, and stop. You are just creating a Dark space. You aren't making the world a better place. You aren't contributing to the betterment of others. You aren't helping others to feel good about themselves. You may think that they can't hear you, but you would be surprised how what you say can be seen, felt, heard, and interpreted, as these are all just frequencies we give off to someone else. You wonder why we have such hostility in the world. Sometimes it's just because we have chosen to label the things in each other that make us different as bad, and thus we create walls. Embrace the things that make us different and allow those things to unite us. Be powerful, wonderful, positive people who can change the world, simply by seeing the Light in the Darkness."

At that moment, I vowed to be more thoughtful about this concept of seeing the Light versus the Darkness in others. I realized that by recognizing Darkness in someone, I wasn't helping to elevate the world in any way. I was only opening up a Dark side in myself. Being a Light in the Darkness recognizes and brings out the powerful, positive things in myself and in others.

That message of being a Light in the Darkness is perhaps one of the most powerful and life-changing lessons I have learned. Living your life each day as a Light changes everything—your interactions, your perspective, your patience, your ability to be resilient, and how you feel about yourself and the world around you.

Spreading the Light

I have a group of fabulous girlfriends who get together each month, no matter what. (Some of these girls are the fitness students I asked to be with me in that first fitness video, and we have been great friends ever since.) We know life gets busy, but we made a pact to free up at least one night a month to see each other and catch up. We take turns planning the month's activity, which usually involves some adventure or outing. I had responsibility for a month in which everyone was extremely busy. The only time I could find for the five of us was on a Sunday for lunch. I made reservations at a local tea-house we had never tried before and asked everyone to wear white. We wanted to celebrate a friend who had overcome cancer, so we wore white in her honor.

When everyone arrived, we chatted a bit, and then I passed around a box of blank note cards. I asked everyone to pick one, and write her name and address on the front of it. I collected the cards and envelopes and then distributed them with the names hidden. I asked each girl to look privately at the name on the envelope and to write a note of gratitude to that person. No rules, just something kind and uplifting. Once they had finished writing their notes, I collected the cards and put them in the mail the next day.

That week I received phone calls from many of the girls, telling me how much it meant to get a card in the mail from one of our pals that spoke words of gratitude. I was surprised how many of the girls said, "I didn't know she thought that way about me—it made my day!"

I didn't realize it at the time, but I had created a similar exercise to the one I participated in as a teenager—and the impact was just as powerful!

Strangers Need Light Too

As I wrote this chapter, I was inspired to see what sort of impact this concept could have with strangers. I created a social media Web event page and invited twelve friends to join it; I encouraged them to invite their friends. It was called 30 Kind Acts in 30 Days. The instructions on the page were simple: "Help to put some light in the world! We are committing to 30 Kind Acts in 30 Days. Feel free to post what you do, or better yet, what someone else did for you to share the positive inspiration!"

I had hoped that a few people would be inspired to join and do something positive in their life and for others. I didn't have any rewards, prizes, or other promotional ploys.

Within seven days, more than 200 people committed to the effort. As I read through the posts, I was excited to see that so many people wanted to put some light into the world and to recognize others who do kind things. The page wasn't boastful or ego-based. Every post seemed to inspire someone else to comment with encouragement. It took no effort to create this—people were naturally drawn to the idea of doing something powerful and positive for each other. The event page turned into an ongoing movement that continues to spread light every day.

Onward, Light Warrior!

A small compliment or act of kindness can make a huge impact on someone's life. I encourage you to do something a little unexpected to bring joy to someone else each day. It doesn't take much, but it can make all the difference to that person, and in return, it can make all of the difference to you as well. People love to feel loved.

As a trusted Light Warrior, I now challenge you to create a Light in the Darkness movement in your life—whether you organize a note-writing campaign, put sticky notes in public places with inspiring messages, create your own webpage for social interaction, or just call a friend. We are brighter when we shine together!

Here are some ways to create your own Light in the Darkness movement:

- Write an affirming, encouraging note and leave it for a friend or family member.

- Write an encouraging note and leave it for a stranger (public bathroom, lunch table).

- Tell someone how much you appreciate him or her.

- Go out of your way to do some good for someone else.

- Do something kind but don't tell anyone—let it be your little secret!

- Leave some breadcrumbs for birds.

- Become a volunteer.

- Shovel, rake, or sweep someone's drive or sidewalk.

- Plan a special get-together with your friends.

- Create a Light in the Darkness exercise.

- Organize a notecard exchange.

- Send someone a card in the mail.

Tying It All Together

Ready to shine? A simple way to begin focusing on this Miracle is to each day ask yourself questions in the following two categories:

- Inspire Yourself: "Was I happy today? Did I celebrate life in some way? Did I find joy despite challenge or difficulty?"

- Inspire Others: "Did someone else have a better day today because of me? Did I help someone to find a more positive out-look? Did I make someone laugh? Did I take the time to make someone else feel good about herself?"

Perhaps you can ask yourself these questions at night as you are praying, meditating, or simply before you go to sleep. If you can say yes to both sets of questions, then I believe you are on the right track to Unlocking the Miracle of Inspiration in your life. If you can't answer in the affirmative, then I ask you to intentionally focus on that area and purposely draw things into your life that will help you to answer "yes!" on a daily basis.

By doing this simple exercise, you are virtually taking a pulse of the overall heartbeat of your soul. Finding personal inspiration every day and bringing inspiration to someone else, every day, may very well be the simplest version of our life purpose.

In yoga, many practices conclude with the word *Namaste*. The general interpretation of this is:

> *May the Light in me honor the Light in you.*
> *May all the good in me honor all the good in you.*
> *May the inspiration in me honor the inspiration in you.*

Go . . . be a Light in the Darkness. Shine on, amazing you! Namaste.

UNLOCK MIRACLE #7 IN YOUR LIFE!

MEDITATION

I INSPIRE. I radiate light—both for myself and for others.

I look for inspiration in each day. I find ways to keep my soul joyful no matter what obstacles get in the way of my day. I surround myself with things and people that bring out the best in me and encourage me to be happy. I pay attention to the little things and big things to make my soul feel energized.

I also look for ways to help other people radiate and find their inspiration as well. Through acts of kindness, a listening ear, or simply taking time for them, I find ways to help people feel good and radiate their own lights.

I give off the energy I want the world to have; I take in the energy my soul needs to be happy. I am a Light Warrior. I am a Light in the Darkness. I INSPIRE.

Journal

Use a journal to record your thoughts and answers. Practice INSPIRING yourself and others.

Be a light in the darkness.

Answer these questions every day, whether during meditation, prayer, or before going to bed.

- ◦ Have you been a Light in the Darkness for yourself today? (Were you inspired today?) What did you do?

- ◦ Have you been a Light in the Darkness for someone else today? (Were you able to bring inspiration to someone else's life today?) What did you do?

REVIEW

INSPIRE YOURSELF

Find inspiration today. Start paying attention to the things in your life that bring you simple joy and happiness. They usually don't cost much (if anything), and they are often already in your life (you just have to look for them). Make a special effort to recognize them in your life every day. Commit to one or two things that you will do each day to nurture your soul. You can select ideas from the following list or come up with your own.

- Listen to music.

- Spend time with a friend.

- Notice something you hadn't noticed before.

- Enjoy being with yourself—read a book, enjoy a sunset, take a walk.

- Make extra time to be with your kids and/or family.

- Plant some flowers or a tree (and water them!).

- Play like a kid.

- Laugh with a friend (or by yourself).

- Love someone unconditionally.

INSPIRE OTHERS

Find ways to nurture someone else's soul. You never know when one small act can change someone's entire energy! You can commit to the same things each day or mix it up, but commit to purposely doing something for someone else every day. You can select from the following list or come up with your own ideas.

- Write an affirming, encouraging note and leave it for a friend or family member.

- Write an encouraging note and leave it for a stranger (public bathroom, lunch table, etc.).

- Tell someone how much you appreciate him or her.

- Go out of your way to do something for someone else.

- Do something kind but don't tell anyone—let it be your little secret.

- Leave some breadcrumbs for the birds.

- Become a volunteer.

- Shovel, rake, or sweep someone's drive or sidewalk.

- Plan a special get-together with your friends.

- Create a Light in the Darkness exercise.

- Organize a notecard exchange.

- Send someone a card in the mail.

   You may find it helpful to write down your inspirations in a journal each day. Looking back on them may motivate you and provide you with ideas for future ways to shine.

The Secret Miracle

Love

The Miracle-Maker

The color of LOVE: White

The scents of LOVE: Anjou Pear, Almond

Everything good comes from Love. Miracles included.
—JULIE

Seven chapters, seven ways to help you unlock the Miracles in your life. Living the 7 Life Miracles is something we practice every day, something that will evolve as we continue to learn and grow. Don't worry about perfecting your Miracles, just invite them into your life every single day. To strengthen your practice, you may want to read the book again, journal about the questions asked throughout, or focus on one Miracle at a time. Let this be the start of an amazing journey.

The 7 Life Miracles open the doors for you to live joyfully, happily, and with confidence. They assist you as you go after what you want, let go of what you don't, and help you find courage and wisdom to know the difference.

Notice I use the terms "open the doors," "assist you," and "help you." That's because the Miracles by themselves can't mobilize your passion and power. You are in the driver's seat, and it is up to you to take these Miracles and use them to live the life your soul desires.

Let's take a moment to look back at our journey together.

THE 7 LIFE MIRACLES

- **EMBRACE** the moment and live urgently. Time doesn't wait for you to be ready. Do it now.

- **CONNECT** with the people in your life in positive and powerful ways. Look for your coaches. Receive the lessons they can give you, and then look for some way to pay them forward. Relationships are essential for a happy soul.

- **CREATE** the masterpiece of your life that you desire. Let go of the past, decide what colors your life is about, and paint them into your every word, thought, and action.

- **EMPOWER** your soul to find happiness first. Nothing else will grant you happiness except the decision to simply be. Whatever energy you give to the world, you will receive in return.

- **CHOOSE** the path, decision, or interpretation that serves you best. Remember that you are never stuck and that you always have choices in your life, in every moment.

- **CLIMB** your mountains with vigor and zest. They are not there as punishment but rather the opposite. The challenges in your life are there to teach you how strong you are and what you really want.

- **INSPIRE** the world. Be a light for yourself and for others every day. Help to build up positive energy in the world. Live a life of inspiration and help someone else do that as well.

These Miracles are with you in the most exciting and the most difficult times. They never waiver; they will never leave you. They are right by your side, as a part of your personal fan club, cheering you on. They are there to help you to be your best—no matter what you are facing.

When you release the 7 Life Miracles into your everyday thoughts and actions, doors open, your Miracles unfold, and you live a bold, powerful, and inspired life. But there's one more thing you should know:

The secret to these Miracles is that they all come from the same place. That's right. All the big things and all the little things; all the unexplained phenomena; all the sensations, powerful changes, and amazing opportunities that open up—everything that happens in your life when you EMBRACE, CONNECT, CREATE, EMPOWER, CHOOSE, CLIMB, and INSPIRE—all tie back into one perfect Miracle.

They all come from LOVE.

Without Love, none of these Miracles could exist. Love is the fabric that binds all of the Miracles together. Love is the success behind everything we do. It is powerful beyond any measure, and it can take an ordinary day and turn it into an extraordinary day. It can take a tough situation and soften it. It can help you live life with joy and passion. It can teach you how to forgive in the darkest moment, or it can teach you to celebrate in the brightest.

Love can heal a broken heart; I know—it healed mine. The doctors tell me I can expect to live a long, good life and that I have a beautiful, healthy heart. At the age of 36, for the first time in my life, my EKG test showed no holes in my heart at all. A Miracle. Love heals all things.

Love is the main ingredient to the 7 Life Miracles.

To truly understand the Miracles, you must welcome Love into your heart. Not some of the time. Not with some people. All of the time. With all people. You must invite Love to speak through your words, through your thoughts, and through your actions. Love is the most important energy you can radiate. It is the intersection point of all the Miracles.

If Love is the intersection point, why didn't I start with it first?

For this reason: It's much like a person who goes on a journey to find something, but discovers they had what they needed all along.

We all are given life with different purposes, passions, and pathways. All of our LifeMaps are designed differently. Some have more twists, some have more turns, some have steeper climbs, and some have deeper valleys. But our end purpose is the same:

♥ To Love ourselves—do something enjoyable, find time to relax, forgive, and let go of the past.

♥ To Love others—do something for someone else without expecting anything in return.

♥ To Love the world—pick up litter, stand up for a cause, buy eco-friendly products, volunteer.

Turn these acts of Love into daily habits. In doing so, you will unlock every one of the 7 Life Miracles.

I LEAVE YOU WITH ONE MORE MEDITATION

Love is the connector to all good things. Love is kind, forgiving, welcoming, and warm. Love has patience. Love comes from reaching out and holding a hand. Love has Light. Love is the most beautiful expression in the world. Love comes from the smiles and laughter of children. Love comes in holding the door for someone—even when inconvenient. Love comes without a price tag or a condition. Love is everything, everywhere, in every person. It is up to me to find Love every day, in all that I do. It is up to me to radiate Love every day, in all that I do. Love heals. Love binds. Love laughs. Love hugs. Love nurtures. My life is about Love.

Unlock all of the Miracles in your life with Love!

Acknowledgments

It is a dream come true to share the messages of the 7 Life Miracles with you. Special thanks to the many people who helped make this possible:

Original design of The 7 Life Miracles symbols: Abraham Cordova

Original edits: Jane Flynn-Royko

Original book formatting: Indie Designz

Cover design: Involve

Photography: Andrew Matre

Final book editing: Shari Johnson

Final book design and typesetting: Gary A. Rosenberg

Publisher: Changing Lives Press

I am grateful for the belief, energy, time, and inspiration from every person who helped make *The 7 Life Miracles* possible. I hope this book serves as one way to pay forward for all of the amazing gifts I have received. Please continue to "pay it forward" and share these messages with others, as one way to continue creating good energy in the world.

Index

About the Author

Julie Wilkes is an author, life coach, motivational lecturer, yoga instructor, fitness presenter, corporate wellness expert, and entrepreneur. She has a master's degree focused on Exercise Physiology from the Ohio State University, and a bachelor's degree in International Business from Marietta College. She is a Registered Yoga Teacher with Yoga Alliance, a certified wellness coach from Wellcoaches, and is a faculty presenter for several nationally accredited fitness organizations. She is the creator of Seven Studios—a yoga, Pilates, barre, boot camp, and life coaching concept whose methodologies are based on the 7 Life Miracles.

Julie has hundreds of fitness and motivational videos and several phone apps. She has developed a series of home and body products based on the 7 Life Miracles. In addition, Julie has designed and managed corporate wellness solutions for a Fortune Global 500 company for more than nine years. She was recognized by *Fitness* magazine as one of the "Top 10 Champions of Health" for 2010, was named a "40 Under 40" award recipient by *Business First*, and is a lululemon athletica ambassador.

Julie is from Columbus, Ohio. She is the proud parent of her three "furry angels," Cody and Charlie (black and tan dachshunds) and Sancho (tuxedo cat).

Julie is a heart disease survivor, and she is passionate about living each day to the fullest and inspiring others to do so as well. She recognizes that she was given a second chance at life, but a second chance is only as good as what she does with it.

The 7 Life Miracles is one of the ways Julie hopes to pay forward on her second chance at life.

To find more on Julie, please visit www.juliewilkes.com.